The God Of Ordinary People

A Spirituality

Sean Caulfield

Sheed & Ward

for Margie and Betty

Scripture references are taken from *The New American Bible*. Washington, D.C. The Confraternity of Christian Doctrine. 1970. Reprinted with Permission.

Other scripture references are from *The New Jerusalem Bible* 1985 by Darton, Longman & Todd, Ltd, and Doubleday & Company, Inc.

Sheed & Ward™ is a service of National Catholic Reporter Publishing Company, Inc.

Library of Congress Catalog Card Number: 88-60115

ISBN: 1-55612-129-6

Published by: Sheed & Ward
            115 E. Armour Blvd., P.O. Box 414292
            Kansas City, MO 64141-4292

To order, call: 800-333-7373

Contents

Introduction

Though the Spirit be one, spiritualities are many. A spirituality is a way of living which emerges from our experience of the Spirit and our response to it. This present work points toward a spirituality for ordinary people, people who are challenged by the turmoils of life. It searches out the sacred in the midst of the secular.

This is a spirituality "from below." It accepts the concrete reality of people's lives and works up from there to their experience of God. This writing accepts this reality, troubled as it very often may be, and explores the underlying hunger and longing for God which it symbolizes and contains. The hunger is often buried beneath unquestioned assumptions about life—that life should be happy, without serious illness, rewarding and ego fulfilling. Reality is otherwise. An untroubled life is an ideal which might be desired; it is not a way of life that is assured. What is constant is the longing for fulfillment, even when the fulfillment seems to elude us. The longing persists despite cultural conditioning or the outworn symbols of religion which served us in our youth. We need to be liberated. But the liberation is not so much from our troubles. What needs a liberation is the hunger of the heart, the longing for the absolute which is at the root of all our troubles.

The format of this writing is not that of a textbook. Its purpose is not to answer questions or give information but to create an atmosphere in which we may get in touch with what ails us and recognize the nature and validity of our longing. It accepts without question or judgment the varied realities of our troubled condition and sees them as the tools furnished by life, or by God, for our growth and creativity.

The central theme of the writing is expressed in a variety of forms in the various chapters. It is that God dwells in radical solitude, that we find God and transcend our troubled state in the acceptance of our own solitude. But God is also an artist who brings forth from the solitude the masterpiece of the universe, the Word enfleshed. In that Word all lesser words are spoken, and the word which is our own life finds its meaning. It is God's genius, the Spirit, which brings that masterpiece to the light and brings us to fulfillment in it. For that reason the acceptance of our solitude is not masochistic but the condition of our creativity.

In the trinity of our ordinary lives, our life's word and our loving talent, the open door to the divine is discovered.

The Way We Are

Though we are troubled, we are called to be beautiful people. Problems refine all that is gross and crass and self-centered in us.

Many of our problems are unavoidable; they come from chance happenings and the limitations of being human. Others are more of our own choosing: obsessions, addictions and phobias. We make the same mistakes, repeat the same patterns of behavior though they destroy our career, our health and the lives of people about us. The human condition is troubled and we need some guidelines to enable us to cope with it.

To be human is to be driven. We experience a need to be more than we are, to transcend ourselves, to seek something greater or more noble. This instinct is at war with all that diminishes us, and it is out of this struggle that all our troubles emerge, whether spiritual, emotional, intellectual or physical. We resist being diminished.

People of faith see this instinct for transcendence as a hunger for God. However, our self-esteem and our need for control do not easily allow us to seek our meaning in God. We avoid our calling, or misunderstand it, while we cast about for something that "works." Once we find that something, we commit ourselves relentlessly to its worship. It rewards us by helping us to forget. It is an anesthetic; it dulls the pain of being troubled people. It might be the inordinate pursuit of money, power, alcohol, food, religion, gambling, sex, health, drugs, spending, sports, approval, perfection, career, another person or an ideal. It works...at first. We enter a quasi-mystical state of self-forgetfulness, a pseudo self-transcendence.

Problems follow because these pursuits are only quick-fix solutions to a hunger that is infinite. There is no finite solution for an infinite hunger. We ourselves become the end product of our worship in our obsessions about the finite.

Many of our troubles arise from a refusal to either drop, or humbly accept, the pain of being human. We prolong the struggle only to find ourselves trapped in the finite. We become what we contemplate: finite, rigid, uptight, unconcerned with the larger world about us. What seemed to work begins to devour us. The millionaire breaks the law in the never-ending pursuit of more wealth. The scientist and believer risk fanaticism in the pursuit of one aspect of truth. The person "wedded to the job" loses family and friends. The person in control engages in covert operations, risks conflict and the love of others because power has become an object of worship. The imperfect person pursues perfection single-mindedly and becomes a hypocrite, intolerant of failure and intolerable to others. Instead of expanding us, our commitment to the finite makes us tense, frustrated and self-destructive. We are all addicted. It is only a matter of degree and of the object of our obsession.

Psychoanalysis has had only partial success in springing the trap of the finite. It has failed in the matter of serious addictions. Behavior Modification and Aversive Conditioning have a string of failures. The way out is the discovery of spiritual power greater than ourselves. This is the secret of the success of Alcoholics Anonymous and of other programs patterned after it. We are made for openness to God. It is not proper that we should be victims of our own self-imprisonment.

That some forms of obsession are socially acceptable—the tireless pursuit of wealth, power, knowledge and self-perfection—does not mean that they are less destructive than those which are socially condemned—the abuse of alcohol, drugs or sex. These things themselves are good, but our human nature rebels when any one of them becomes an end in itself. When we are sick we look for a cure. But there is no prescription for our deepest troubles. A pre-scription means something written ahead of time, a ready-made solution. We may never say that we have a solution to our problems in advance of their arrival. Our hope lies in an openness to the mystery of our existence as it unfolds. What we shall do and who we shall be in the future we do not know. All we know is that there is no partial solution or prescription, be it alcohol, a promotion or a check, for our ordinary condition.

Our hunger is for the absolute, and our troubles alert us to this hunger. An aspirin may ease a headache; it cannot ease the heartache. The heart needs a love which has no boundaries. The remedy is spiritual. That does not mean that there are not more immediate solutions to practical problems. We give food to starving people, not advice to pray. What it means is that in the long haul—though all be fed, healthy and educated—the hunger of heart remains, the spirit is starving.

Our spirit has a fragmented view of reality. This results in a fragmented attitude to the world about us leading to stress, failure and prejudice. It is not that we have any choice about being troubled at times. But our fragmented self can be united only through an encounter with an absolute good. While we accept the reality of our troubled state, we can still know that it is possible to transcend it. We may hope for a spiritual experience and for a higher power to free us.

Freedom is bought with some pain. Giving up something, or letting go of someone to whom we are attached, is painful. Even if the pain is great, it does not necessarily mean that our love is great. All it means is that our addiction is great. To overcome this pain it is helpful to discover the symbolical meaning of our attachment.

All the attachments with which we struggle are symbolical as well as real. Alcohol may mean the uninhibited freedom of the spirit (it is well-named: "spirits"); food may mean a reward we allow ourselves; obsession with money may mean security; being wedded to the job may mean a need for creativity of the spirit; an obsession with another person may express a fear of being alone. We are never alone. The discovery of the symbolical meaning will enable us to seek fulfillment on a higher level.

Some of our troubles arise from the belief that we are unlovable or inadequate. We should forgive ourselves for being unlovable, inadequate, mistaken or even potbellied. Our brokenness is proper to the human condition. The real truth is that life itself is vastly more than any experience of being unloved. It is more than the meaningless suffering we experience, the inadequacy or the regretted sinfulness. It takes strength and courage to accept this, courage combined with slow and determined effort. What God calls us to is growth and maturity. Growth takes time and effort. With a little courage and much humility it is possible for us to be complete persons without the false crutches we think we need.

Our search for meaning does not begin with pat answers but with the concrete reality of our lives. Our search or hunger or longing should be recognized for the wonderful and challenging thing it is. It is our call to be creative, refined and beautiful people.

What To Do

Purpose: To discover that only the Infinite can satisfy you.

Share: What "stuff" is important to you.
What "stuff" you think you could survive without.
What ready-made prescriptions you have to enable you to cope with stress.

Music: Pachelbel's *Canon,* Cassette tape Everest 3462.

Quiet time: Reflect on what it would be like to be destitute, as many Third World people are.
Open your heart to God who alone can fill it.

End: Pray aloud Psalm 103.

God In Exile

There are many ways besides geographically of being in exile. A person may be in emotional exile—left out, passed by, unloved; in spiritual exile—not knowing how to relate to God or make sense of life; in religious exile—at odds with the established churches; in intellectual exile—misunderstood by petty minds, deprived of worthwhile literature. In this chapter exile means any or all of these. Such exiles leave us troubled people.

Theologically speaking, God dwells in perpetual exile. This is a Jewish insight emerging from their lived experience. The question was asked: "If God be All, how can anything other than God exist?" The reply they gave, simplistic enough in itself, was that God went into exile so that what is other than God might come into existence. To be a Chosen People meant being found within the exile of God. This is the meaning of Egypt, Babylon, the destruction of the Temple, the loss of the schechinah, the ghettos of Europe, Russia and America. It is out of their exile in God that they give the world knowledge of God, of the Law and the prophets. Their existence within God is a mission for the religious and cultural enrichment of all the nations of their exile.

God lives in perpetual exile. God is "other." Christians say that God came to them out of the exile, without ever abandoning it, in the person of

5

Jesus of Nazareth. The Word, proceeding from the Father, was sent into exile on earth: "As the Father has sent me" (Jn 20:21). The Word is sent into exile as a person in his own right, sent on a mission to the world. The Spirit is sent by the Word from its home in the Trinity:

"If I go,
I will send him to you" (Jn 16:7).

The Father cannot be sent, but may come:

"Anyone who loves me
will be true to my word,
and my Father will love him;
we will come to him
and make our dwelling place with him" (Jn 14:23).

It is out of our own exile, our experience of this solitude of God, that all our creative enrichment of others emerges. As long as we are comfortable and unchallenged nothing gets changed, there is no growth. Comfort is the breeding ground of delay. We need the exile, which is a way of saying that we need to be moved off-center and have our assumptions challenged. We ask, "Where do I go from here? What must I do?"

This questioning is the beginning of our spiritual journey. The journey has its horrors as well as its spiritual purpose. The horrors have to be confronted: loneliness, feelings of rejection, the absence of God, alcoholism, divorce, being strangers in a strange environment. The presence of all these troubles, and many more, is evidence enough of the exile in people's lives. The spiritual purpose of the exile is that we should have a change of heart and return to our Father's home. We do this when we accept our exile, beget the real masterpiece of our personal existence by being co-creators of our future with God's help.

Exile is not a punishment. It is hardly even a test, though it is that. It is a call to growth. If we remain in one place, at one level of development, we remain impoverished, very often narrow and childish in our view of reality. We remain culturally isolated. It is not proper to think that the culture which has been ours from birth must be the norm for the rest of the world.

Exile enriches us if we cleanse our eyes and rid ourselves of our unreasonable fears of who and what is strange in other cultures and religions. When other nationals move among us we are all enriched. When we are in trouble we have the possibility of an entirely new future. It is a serious impoverishment to close our eyes to our possibilities, to other ways of thinking and doing things, to other religions and political systems. These experiences are needed for wholeness, for the salvation of the whole person.

Exile and Theology

It is out of exile, out of a hunger for fullfillment that all our God-talk surfaces. The exile of women from the social and religious fields gives us the beginnings of a Christian feminist theology. The exile of black people in their experience of discrimination gives us black theology. The exile of the poor and oppressed from their place in society gives us liberation theology. We have to listen to all of them, or we shall find ourselves spiritually malnourished. It is from the disharmony in troubled people's lives that all wondering about God comes to light. It is this wondering which enables us to understand the "signs of the times," to come home to our true meaning and to form bonds of unity.

Theologies are formed and developed through symbols and stories. In the case of exile it may be Jacob at the ford of Jabbock, Moses crossing the sea of reeds, the Hindu crossing the Perilous Bridge, the Navaho warrior crossing the rainbow, or the migrant crossing the Rio Grande. They are Christ among us because the real exile is within, a journey of conversion from the less desirable into completeness and spiritual maturity.

The religious journey involves risk and trials; it is a perilous journey. The Jews have a story for it:

> Once upon a time, four talmudic sages went on the mystical journey to Paradise. They were Ben Azai, Ben Zoma, Aher (Elisha Ben Avuya) and Rabbi Akiva. Ben Azai gazed and died. Ben Zoma gazed and went mad. Aher became a heretic. Rabbi Akiva came out in peace.

The story reminds us that those who are on the spiritual journey of exile need discernment, good judgment, fearlessness and decision. Only those, like Rabbi Akiva, who have made the journey may say with some measure of insight what should be done to heal our troubled state. A government official, a theologian or a troubled person who is unwilling to accept solitude has little to offer the world.

God went into exile, making room for the Word, lest the divine smother in radical solitude.

The Word was sent into exile in incarnation to save all other words from being smothered in the finite.

The Spirit was sent to make us universal in the religious sense lest we smother in the womb of comfort, in the narrow views of one culture, one theology, one political viewpoint, one art, one literature or one way of thinking. Nothing that is true or good is foreign to God. It should not be foreign to God's people. We enter the foreign country of Judaism, Zen, Tantrism, Hinduism and the Muslim world to learn there what the universality of God is all about. All the fruits of the human spirit are fruits of the Holy Spirit. We embrace the exile so as to save and be saved, to have our eyes opened to God.

The exile is vital because our psyche is universal in its needs. Its opening is on infinity. If it is cheated of that opening, if it is habitually focused on one interest only, our life becomes narrow. It matters not that such an interest might be of vital importance. We are all familiar with religious cranks and with people who can speak and think of only one interest. When we allow this to happen to us, our spiritual and psychological life rebels. This rebellion reveals itself in some form of obsession or prejudice. This manner of being "possessed" makes us very troublesome people indeed. It has the power to destroy us. It is the price of our not going, or of our not being allowed to go, into exile. The obsessions, fanaticisms and phobias, whether about religion, race, politics or salvation, are a warning that our spirit needs an outlet. It longs for the richness of what is good and authentic in other ways of life. The human spirit longs for what is universal.

Our model of accepted exile is the Word of God. That Word proclaimed without fanaticism, fear or obsession that we should prepare in our solitude a way for the Lord. It came into exile in our world, revealed in the person of Jesus of Nazareth, yet was never absent from its home in the Trinity. It ascended into exile from its home in the world, yet never abandoned it. St. Augustine writes:

For he did not linger, but hastened away,
crying out by his words and deeds, his life and death,
his descent and ascension,
crying out to us to return to him.
And he vanished from our eyes
that we should return to our own heart and find him there,
For he went away, and behold he is here.
He willed not to be long with us, and yet he did not leave us,
for he returned whence he had never departed,
because the world was made by him.
Since life has descended, will you not ascend and live? (*Confessions*
LV:12).

Exile and Body

The call to exile begins with the insight that there must be something greater and better, that meaning is never found in seeking ourselves.

Troubled people may cross an ocean or river, symbolically speaking, yet never burn their boats. They never really embrace the exile. This is tragic because little is learned and little shared. Whatever the exile—spiritual, emotional, geographical, religious or other—there is always a temptation to make a selection from what was best and most loved in the past, erect it into a myth and proceed to live in it as if it were the whole of reality. A fired or rejected person fails to move on; a hurt person fails to forgive; a religious person fails to seek out a deeper meaning. The myths of the Irish-American are wholly foreign to those of the homeland. The homeland moved on. The colonial British became a caricature of those they left behind in England. The educated and wealthy Jews of Babylon and New York had dreams of establishing a sovereign nation again, but most had sense enough not to return there when return was possible. Exiles who weave myths of the past, whether post-Irish, post-British, post-Vatican II, post-matrimony or post-modern, have not burned their boats behind them.

Jesus burned his boats.

Though he was in the form of God, he did not regard equality with God something to be grasped at. Rather, he emptied himself (Phil 2:6,7).

It was for this reason that God raised him on high and made him whole in resurrection. Not that we should turn our backs on the past, but rather that we should refuse to live in it. Whatever the nature of our troubled state, we must look to the future. Growth into God comes when we accept our new challenging situation objectively.

We go into exile the day we accept responsibility for the real meaning of our lives and go in search of it. All protests against the abuse of power, civil and ecclesiastical, against greed, racism, ignorance and despair are steps on our journey into the exile of God. Those who are comfortable with the world as it is are a challenge to us to move out into the exile of the spirit. We are the stewards of the earth, not its consumers. The consumers want ever more and become aggressive. The exile of the Word was tragic in Jesus of Nazareth because he opposed our devouring one another. It is a journey full of danger. But all efforts for peace, justice, reconciliation, economic and educational well-being for the less fortunate are steps on our journey home to God who is within us. When we love others, as only they can be loved in their concrete bodily and historical reality, God is loved and the pain of exile ends.

The migrations of people are a search for God. People even search the skies. The poor, the exploited and the explorers go into exile because there must be something better. That something, when the search is finished, is God, the only future coming toward us. "Out of darkness light shall shine;" out of solitude, creativity; out of demographic, emotional or spiritual compression, emanation. And yet when the hunger is satiated we have only come back to our true self: the reign of God within.

Those who accept their exile in the strange land of personal troubles will find that the terrors of the exile are only a crucifixion for the sake of the reign of God. The God of the lonely, the alcoholic, the abused or the migrant is in their hearts, nowhere else. God has been born in so many caves and stables, labor camps and ghettos; has crossed so many Rio Grandes and oceans; has been sold into so many black and white slaveries; has been crucified in so many sweatshops, onion fields and apple orchards. Those in exile know quite well who it is: the God of the poor and troubled who cannot be accepted by a world closed in on itself. The power of God gives meaning to the troubled in their solitude.

José

When José came across the river, he felt that he had entered the Promised Land. There would be meat on the table and money to spend. The reality he found was a state of semi-slavery guaranteed and protected by custom and law.

His patron, a wealthy potato farmer, paid off the "coyote" (the guide for his illegal entry) and hired him. On wet days, when there is no need to move irrigation pipes, José gets no pay. Nor will he have work when winter comes. When he needs groceries he goes to the store and charges them to the patrón who withholds their cost, as he did that of the "coyote," from his paycheck. José lives in a broken-down trailer with his wife and two children, his two brothers and their friend. The rent and utilities are withheld from his paycheck. Occasionally, the employer will withhold a tithe for the employer's church. Every five years or so José gets lonely for the homeland and the sight of his parents. The "coyote" is advanced the money for the trip. It is withheld from his paycheck.

At the end of each year José still has no money. He has no hope of getting out of the cycle of poverty, or of getting decent living quarters. However he is never without a smile. He speaks to me of the hopelessness of it all—the minimal wage, the bleak future—and still he smiles. The patrón congratulates himself profusely in my presence for the good care he is giving at their door as they speak. I am not invited in. I am distracted by the thought that they also take good care of their dog. José invites all of us into this trailer. His compadres *like to visit, and we laugh a lot. Everybody is pressed to eat in a trailer which is spotless despite the poverty.*

The solitude of God is exiled within the heart of José and has come to know itself as the God of the poor. José has come to know the freedom of the children of God.

I led you for forty years in the desert.
Your clothes did not fall from you in tatters
nor your sandals from your feet; bread was not your food,
nor wine or beer your drink.
Thus you should know that I, the Lord, am your God (Dt 29:4-5).

José knows this. That is why he is smiling.

What To Do

Purpose: To get in touch with your exile and find God there.

Share: Where you were born. What is special about you because of your place of birth?
What was your experience of leaving home or leaving the area of your birth?
Share the experience of being "out of it" spiritually or emotionally.

Music: Samuel Barber's *Adagio for Strings,*
Columbia/Odyssey 33230.

Quiet time: With eyes closed, make a home within you for God. Experience coming home to the Father.

End: Pray aloud psalm 84.

The Prayers Of Ordinary People

There are problems which are not of our own making and not of God's making either. They come from no other source than life itself, life in an unfinished world. In a moral sense they are neither good nor bad. What we do with them, however, will diminish us or fulfill us.

There are other problems which are of our own making. We have a choice here also: to make an identity out of our misery or, with God's help, choose to be healed.

In either case, how we think about God and whether or not we pray will determine the outcome.

Sifting Out Our Concept of God

When God reveals the inner working of the divine to us, it is always the unvarnished truth. The basic content of that truth is that we are loved personally and absolutely—no strings attached. God does not play games. The love that is offered to us is not conditioned by our response to it or by our neglect of it. God's love is always available to us.

If we have been indoctrinated with the concept of a judgmental God, we hide our true meaning lest we incur criticism or rejection. But hiding our true meaning from God makes us lonely. We lose touch not only with God but with ourselves also. This results in all forms of spiritual and emotional problems, problems brought on by anxiety and lack of love. We develop a reluctance to know and be known lest knowledge reveal to us the things we so not wish to see.

When we lose touch with the living and true God, we end up with a monster of our own making: a god who is unpredictable, given to favoritism, erratic and capable of all manners of prejudice. God becomes, like the gods of Mount Olympus, a projection of all our worst selves. We then feel a compulsion to engage in some form of magic to appease him, or we turn away. Religious worship becomes a superstitious insurance policy against this vengeful god. We begin to fulfill obligations with a mentality which insists that what really matters is the obligation and its fulfillment. It takes the place of what would have been a joyful response of love and life to a God who is Mother as much as Father to us, who is wisdom, lover and savior.

The God of the legalistic person is almighty, judgmental and vindictive. This God expects people to be perfect and to be in control of their feelings and thoughts. Broken people—we are all broken—with this concept of God hide a true self which would have wept, acknowledged the brokenness and been spontaneous. When they fail, as inevitably they must, they expect punishment. This forces them to turn away in their deepest self even when they continue their outward observance. They struggle to maintain a false image of a perfect self, a struggle which takes great spiritual energy. Such people are unable to live up to the expectations they project onto God. As a result, they are unable to be sincere with themselves. Not only does life lose its meaning and despair creep up on them, but their values deteriorate and their deeds betray them. They become imprisoned within themselves with God as their jailer.

We are tempted to avert our eyes in prayer lest we see what is in the eyes of God. And we lower our eyes lest God sees what is in our own eyes: our pettiness, anger, greed, suspicion, duplicity, indifference. Were we to

look into God's eyes in prayer we would see into depths that are un-
fathomable. We would become what we see: open with wonder, deep with
understanding and gentle with compassion. We should never fear this encounter because, no matter who or what we are, we are wholly acceptable
to God.

> Can a mother forget her infant,
> be without tenderness for the child of her womb?
> Even should she forget,
> I will never forget you (Is 49:15).

The God who loves ordinary people suffers with them. "Only a God
who suffers can save us," Bonhoeffer said. A sincere openness to the God
who loves us to the point of passion and death promotes inner peace and
health.

The God who loves us knows us. We long to be known, not only from
the outside but from within. We want to be known by someone who really
loves us. We feel that if others knew us as we really are, with our hopes,
dreams and struggles to be whole, they would have a compassionate and
tolerant love for us. Conversely, were we to live for an hour within the
mind of another, even that of a social outcast, we would come away
humbled and more understanding. We cannot know people from within,
only from without and with difficulty despite our love. Not so with God.
The Spirit of God has been poured out on us (Acts 10:45). We know God
and are known from within. God has made a home in us (Jn 14:23). This is
our experience of prayer. We are those who "have the mind of Christ" (1
Cor 2:16). "For, to me 'life' means Christ" (Phil 1:21), Paul writes. Once
we have sifted out a truer concept of God there are no barriers to communication—just evasions.

When we disclose our hearts to God, prayer becomes an adventure. It
tells us who the living God is. It helps us to live the life of God from within
despite our troubled condition.

Disclosing the Heart

When we say to someone, "Hello, I'm John Doe," we seldom get the reply, "Who cares?" Even those who do not care respond with their own name. Just as anger begets anger and laughter begets laughter, so disclosure begets disclosure. God has already disclosed the innermost life of the divine to us as love. The purpose is to get us to disclose our hearts with a like love.

There is, of course, no way in which troubled people can be forced, by God or by anyone else, to disclose their hearts. Neither can God be forced. It is a matter of invitation. In our prayer God invites us to open our hearts in trust. We invite God to do likewise. God does not manipulate us. The divine does not do things "to teach us a lesson." Neither can we manipulate God. Two freedoms encounter each other in trust and mutual respect. Anything may happen in this encounter.

When we open our troubled hearts to God, God in turn reveals something to us. This may not remove the troubling condition or event, but it will make it endurable. We cannot say what it is that God will disclose. It depends on the kind of personality we have, and on what it is that disturbs us. God responds to each individual in the manner which is suitable to that person. Nor may we expect quick-fire responses to our cries for help. We have to develop the capacity to receive God. We have for so long not listened. Becoming tuned-in to recognize how God acts in us is a slow process.

> For my thoughts are not your thoughts,
> nor are your ways my ways, says the Lord.
> As high as the heavens are above the earth,
> so high are my ways above your ways
> and my thoughts above your thoughts (Is 55:8-9).

People complain that when they listen to God there is only silence. That silence may be a problem for some. We know that if God discloses nothing to our listening, we are betrayed. But betrayal is not possible. We must look deeper. God's silence forces us to go on considering and disclosing until an insight dawns on us. It takes time for the heart to open. God speaks to a disclosed heart, not to a closed one.

We approach God with trust. We know that our trust will never be violated or used against us. If we trust God—and trust is what is demanded of us in our troubled life—God will reveal a lover's heart to us. We shall find ourselves understood from within, supported, loved with compassion.

We may question God. That is proper since we are persons. We will find that God turns the question around and asks for sincerity. In these disclosures we come to know ourselves, our good and our bad, our strength and our vulnerability.

We are vulnerable because many of us, perhaps most, have been victimized in one manner or other, at one time or another. It may have been by people who took advantage of us or abused their power. It may have been by circumstances beyond anyone's control. We are even victims of our culture. We have been lied to and propagandized by the media, the military, the advertisers, the manufacturers and people in high places. Perhaps we have become shrewd and protective. We may find it difficult to open our hearts. Yet the most healthy thing in life is to become like little children again in our trusting relationship with God. It is there that we find meaning for our troubled condition. This happens when we pray, listening in silence, allowing our hearts to expand. We clear the noise out of our minds and listen when he speaks. Time and again, in Isaiah, Proverbs and Psalms, God invites us to listen:

Come, children, hear me (Ps 34:12).
Hear, O daughter, and see; turn your ear
forget your people and your father's house.
So shall the king desire your beauty (Ps 45:11).
Hear, O children, a father's instruction (Prv 4:1).

If our problems are phony and self-serving, they deserve God's silence. Some problems are the result of years of insincerity. God's silence is a challenge to that insincere approach to life. If we refuse to forgive those who have hurt us, to listen and respond to them or extend a helping hand, we make it impossible for God to speak to us. God is found through others.

God speaks to us very often through the remembered words and actions of another. There are people who perceive everything in terms of themselves. What does not feed into their self-interest is overlooked as irrelevant; they do not even hear us. Such people are tiresome to themselves and to others. They bore us to death and they themselves experience a large measure of frustration. This frustration comes from soliciting people's approval and praise. It leads to further emotional and physical troubles. God is not in the business of furthering this form of egotism.

We may have played such games with ourselves and others, refused to look issues straight in the face, avoided the obvious steps we know we should have taken. This makes hypocrites of us. This is a painful truth which must be confronted. When we have a problem we should not maintain a phony exterior, especially in the sight of God. If we have sinned we should not try to rationalize it away. If we have been sinned against, we should be angry, perhaps weep, until such time as we are able to forgive. Jesus has compassion on all manner of sinful and troubled people. But there was one brand of sinner for whose actions he had no use: the hypocrite. Hypocrites never disclose their true identity. They do not want to grow or change. They do not invite love because they are "in control." Their world is legal and finite. Fulfilling obligations gives them security. The obligations become more important than people. Troubled people, the poor, the minorities, as well as creative ideas and new ways of doing things, threaten them. Though they do not know it, they are in fact full of fear. But they do not believe or acknowledge that they are troubled. They cannot be forgiven or healed because they are unaware of any need for forgiveness or healing; they cannot express compassion because compassion would admit that the world is not as they insist it should be. There is some of that hypocrisy in all of us and it disturbs our praying.

If we but sit and listen to God, God will heal our disorder. People who acknowledge their ordinary state and their struggles with it are close to God's idea of a human person called to greatness.

Everyone needs to be close to at least one other person, God or a friend, or God as friend. Hell is no more than the absence of friends. God's friendship is always available to people in prayer. Prayer is a disclosure which results in friendship. It has nothing to do with the roles we play. We frequently hear people identifying themselves through the roles they play in life: "I'm a teacher." "I'm a housewife." "I work at the bank." The roles we play tell us nothing of who we really are. They have no place in our conversation with God. What we do in prayer is struggle in silence to uncover our depths, our inner mystery. It is a process of discovery. We use everything—ideas, memories, fantasies, symbols—to enable ourselves to open up to infinity. We disclose ourselves in the manner a rose discloses its beauty to the sky. A rose is a rose not by playing a role but by offering the beauty and fragrance of what it is to those who love roses. This is what the average person is trying to do in prayer: slowly opening up and disclosing to God and to others the inner depths and beauty of who he or she is. The person is healed by friendship when God and others love and accept this hidden beauty.

Here is where sincerity is important. Belittling ourselves before God is an untruth. It does not reveal the whole person. We quietly accept the mystery and dignity of our humanness, whatever our failings may be. Wallowing in guilt feelings must be nauseating to a God who wants us to accept love and the joy of friendship. It is not so much our reality as troubled people as our sincerity which needs correction. We have creative ideas. We have fears and doubts. It takes a great deal of courage to act on our ideas. We may, after all, fail and be hurt again—hence the fears and doubts. But if we do not act on our ideas we betray ourselves. Our creative ideas always come from the center of our being. Not to act on our convictions is to be insincere with ourselves.

Every troubled person has difficulty knowing what life is all about, what meaning it has. We wonder whether we should hope or despair. We find our wisdom when we open our hearts to God and listen for a like disclosure from God. Stress decreases, insights emerge, decisions are made and the courage to be beautiful people develops. Troubled but sincere people always have a wisdom and beauty which the complacent lack.

What To Do

Purpose: To sift out a better concept of God.

Share: How you thought of God as a child.
                The ways in which your thinking about
                God has changed.
                Do you ever experience God as silent or indifferent?

*Background
music:*   Vaughan Williams' *The Lark Ascending*, CVA 25020.

Quiet time: Focus attention deep within your spirit.
                Let your heart open to God the way a rose
                opens to those who love roses.
                Disclose your deepest and true self.

End: Pray aloud the Magnificat, Luke 1:46-55.

The Place For Love

Loosely put, the Greeks had the idea that what makes one a person is knowledge. If we know ourselves, we have power. We control our destiny. The greater the knowledge, the greater our power and control over others. We are revealed in the company of others as strong personalities. There is a destructive sort of truth in this, but it is certainly not biblical.

The biblical idea differs. In the biblical way of thinking, personality is determined by the free gift of oneself. Personality does not come from knowledge but from freedom. Each person is a center of freedom which is inviolate and beyond the reach of others. From this center of personal freedom we may make the gift of ourselves to others, "lay down our lives for them." The more we serve the needs of others, the more personality we have. Hell is isolation from others, irrespective of the knowledge we might have. Heaven is the total gift of self. It is a state of absolute loving. The growth of a troubled person consists in the development of a loving relationship with God which allows this center to be free.

It might be said that in the one God there are three centers of freedom, the freedom of the solitude to reveal itself, the freedom of the revealed Word to lay down its life and take it up again (Jn 10:18), and the freedom of the Spirit to "blow where it will" (Jn 3:8). In our search, we are called to the center of those freedoms. God invites us to come freely out of our solitude and isolation and reveal our inner mystery to others to be free enough to lay down our lives for them, and to be creative in whatever manner the Spirit inspires us. This is the place for love. This is the manner in which we share the inner mystery of who God is. This is done with, in and through God's own freedom which is within us. It is God's freedom which invites us to love freely and not from necessity, to trust and surrender our lives. The freedom to love is the enrichment of our inner center of being.

Because a personal center is free, it is a mystery. Mystery may be explored, but it cannot be commanded or fully comprehended. We cannot be compelled to come out of our solitude and love. We are invited. Love does not compel. "Here I stand, knocking at the door. If anyone hears me calling and opens the door, (then) I will enter his house and have supper with him, and he with me" (Rv 3:20). Not that the mystery and the freedom would then cease to exist. If the center of mystery ever ceased to be beyond our grasp, God would cease to be God, and we would lose interest. While love thrives on mystery, mystery invites love.

Ordinary people take themselves in hand the day they choose to respond to God's invitation to love. What exactly we mean when we say that we love God is not easy to explain. It is not sentimentality, though love does touch our deepest reality and tears may flow at first. To say that we love God means that in the totality of our being, in our deepest meaning, we live for God. It also means that in God's totality the divine life and love is ours. Love to be perfect must be mutual. It means allowing God to be free in our regard, active and alive, a mystery and a challenge. It means accepting and being enriched by the disclosure of God's deepest self to us. This was the love which enriched and consoled Paul, enabling him to write:

> Praised be God, the Father of our Lord Jesus Christ, the Father of mercies, and the God of all consolations! He comforts us in all our afflictions and thus enables us to comfort those who are in trouble, with the same consolation we have received from him (2 Cor 1:3-4).

This love brings consolation, not always a solution or end to our troubles. But it also brings enrichment. It makes us more alive, more capable of the gift of ourselves and better able to cope with life.

When we love others we have a natural desire to know more about them, what it is that motivates them, how they experience themselves from within. Our love for God has that same desire. It is a subtle thing, done with reverence and receptiveness. What we seek is a personal knowledge of God, not information about the divine. There can be few expectations in this situation. Expectations kill love and shackle freedom. The God we love will always surprise us. Expectations leave little room for surprises. Though the divine may be immutable in its own regard, with respect to us God is always changing, always free. The surprise is that the God of our childhood is not the God of our troubled years. As our experience of God expands our freedom, our love for God grows and changes. From the free center of our being we are invited to choose love in more creative ways.

Our love expands our heart to other people. It compels us to work for love on a one-to-one basis as well as to struggle for the well-being of all. In a world in which there are many oppressed and poor people this will often entail standing at the foot of the cross watching Christ die there. When we have done everything possible, the body of Christ still hangs there. We know that we cannot take it down or alleviate its pain. "The poor we shall have always with us." But this should help us to see our troubles in perspective. It should enable us to allow them shrink to their proper proportions.

The God we love respects our hurt. God did not cause it. Sometimes the hurt remains because enduring it enables people to grow. But the hurt itself is an evil; a physical, not a moral, evil. Sometimes it is removed because it is an obstacle to our loving God who, we may well presume, wishes to remove whatever prevents the free flow of our love. Not every hurt is an obstacle to loving, but when it is we should cooperate with God in its removal. In either case, God's love for us is not diminished.

God does not patronize us or belittle us. The reason is that true love either finds, equals or creates them. Since we are not God's equals, God stoops down to us in our troubled state:

> I myself taught Ephraim to walk,
> I took them in my arms;...
> I led them with reins of kindness,
> with leading-strings of love.
> I was like someone who lifts an infant close against his cheek;
> stooping down to him I gave him his food (Hos 11:3-4, *JB*).

God became our equal in the troubled Word-made-flesh:

> (He) emptied himself
> to assume the condition of a slave,
> and became as men are;
> and being as all men are,
> he was humbler yet,
> even to accepting death,
> death on a cross (Phil 2:7-8, *JB*).

This love of equals is not a love which satisfies vanity or self-interest. What it does is inspirit people with the Holy Spirit of Christ which was handed over on the cross, poured out on Pentecost. It is a love which brings fortitude, wisdom, comfort and awe. It is not a wishy-washy sentimental high. Highs come from addictions which eventually betray us. God does not fail us; God's love is patient. If we rebel, God does not turn away. If we get angry with God, God awaits our understanding. If we are weak, we are invited to humility and the re-making of our inner life. God offers us all the beauty of the world so that we have no need to covet what does not belong to us. God was tempted in the person of Jesus as we are tempted. Like us in everything, Jesus struggled. He did not sin because he chose not to sin. That is God's freedom.

Ordinary people struggle in their loving to be freed from the gods of this world which tell us that to be whole we must conform, be successful, wealthy, powerful and young. We do not have to be whole persons in that sense. What love does is invite us to surrender our lives in freedom and trust to God's love. God's love is tough love, challenging us to grow. But it is faithful: "And know that I am with you always; yes, to the end of time" (Mt 28:20, *JB*). The temptation which Jesus turned down was to abandon love for control that is the risk, not rejection, not absorption but the exercise of power.

Experiencing God's Love

"Do you know God?"

People reply, "Oh, sure. I know who God is." Then they proceed to offer information. But knowing God is less a matter of information and more a matter of experience and love.

The experience of God is a process: a flow of intuitions, memories, feelings, subliminal understandings, fantasies and the perceptions of people and things which lead us to the ground of our being.

Some people experience things more intensely than others. They are the great artists and lovers. Some have little or no reaction to the mysteries of the world about them—for them, everything is explained. Creative people have intense perceptions and as a result intense troubles at times. To experience what no other person perceives is to set oneself up for contradiction. Look what happened to Jesus of Nazareth! It is the price a person pays for the touch of God's Spirit in mind, body, memory, imagination and creative talent. God's touch makes us passionate in our love for people, things and events. Passion is needed to create or love well. In our experience of a loving God, creativity and apathy struggle together. Out of the struggle comes the creation of our inner being, what we shall be forever. We struggle with the stupidities of life until a breakthrough occurs, an insight which makes the meaningless meaningful. This is the loving of troubled people.

What one person experiences of God is not the experience of another. An experience is personal. It depends on who we are, what our experience of life has been and the symbol system through which we perceive what is other than ourselves. The reality of God is vastly greater than anything our minds can comprehend. To open ourselves to an experience of God we have to develop a large and loving spirit. We set ourselves to be sensitive to all that is mystery. We search the world about us so as to comprehend.

No experience of the mystery or the love of another, even of God, is a final answer to our search. Final answers breed fanaticism. Rather, such an experience is the beginning of a better question. It leads us deeper into the mystery. One positive aspect of our troubles is that they force us to ask those questions, only to leave us surprised by what we discover—the personal love of God for us. Information may well tell us that God is a God of love, but information never converted anyone. The love we discover is infinitely greater than any love we have for ourselves. Authentic growth occurs when our experience of being loved enables us to break out of the controls our fears place on us. We are able to move on. It takes courage to choose the future, to move on rather than remain bogged down in the present or the past. But a decision like this establishes our worth as human persons. It is a revolutionary moment, a moment of self-transcendence made possible by the security we have in the experience of God's love for us. That love heals the wounds our troubles inflicted.

When our troubles are excruciating, they have no simplistic answer. What answer there is can be found only in the tough love of God. It is contained in whatever response the Father made to the Son when he prayed: "My God, my God, why have you forsaken me?" (Mk 15:34). The response lay in being drawn through death into the solitude of the Father so as to be poured out in resurrection into the lives of all who accept him. Our troubles call us into communion with all fragile and hurting people as they share the passion and resurrection of Christ. It is a call to love, to know the abandoned heart of Christ, the solitude of the Father, the inexhaustible outpouring of the Spirit. It is not a call to despair, to the dead end of imprisonment within ourselves. This experience of God's love can be a frightening thing. But it is inherent in our experience of trouble. It is a share in the life, love and destiny of God's Son.

Privacy

Only love can heal our troubled hearts. The deepest and most authentic expression of that love is always private. Privacy is part of all that is sacred in our life and in our love for God. What is sacred is always treated with reserve. Since love is mutual, perhaps one reason for privacy is the risk of rejection. We oftentimes hide our love of others even in the very deeds which express it. We are cautious. To have exposed our soul only to have that disclosure treated with casualness, indifference or amusement is a devastating experience. We also have the fear of being absorbed by others. The risk exists because it is difficult to communicate our deepest mystery. An experience of love may be shared or discussed, but the reality always remains private. Then again, our self-revelations are so fumbling at best, even when our love is sincere. We need privacy.

We cannot tell our problems to the whole world. Even with a friend, tears may flow. We are embarrassed. We do not know why things have to be the way they are. And the friend who accepts our disclosure is so unprepared for it all. We end up apologizing—even to God. But if our love is great enough to allow us to express our troubles in private, we feel better. We appreciate the other's silence. All we needed was an understanding heart. We should have some reservation, however, in telling our troubles to someone who has never been hurt, or to one whose lifestyle is control rather than compassion.

We may misunderstand God's silence at first, but we come to appreciate the space it gives us. Words are banal when we hurt, which is why God says so little. God has been hurt. All troubled people need is reassurance, even when they "feel a fool for having bothered you." It is no bother to God to listen. It should not be to the rest of us.

It is helpful to find a private place once we decide to bring our hurt to God. It should be away from the crowds and the noise. It might be a favorite room when the house is empty, a place by the river or lake or a quiet corner in church. We sit there with God, putting the misery within Christ's experience of pain. What is disclosed to us there is private. It would make little sense to another person. It is in this private place that we come to know who we are ourselves, who we are to God and who we should be to other people. These moments of getting away from it all give us the opportunity to assess our troubles in an objective manner.

Privacy sharpens our perception of ourselves. The difference between a troubled person tempted to suicide and a troubled person invited to love and growth is the person's perception of himself or herself. Some people believe that nothing can change, that they are abandoned to themselves. It is a feeling of despair. It is true nothing can change so long as we do nothing. But to embark on a new venture always changes the way we see the world and ourselves. The minimum in this new venture is to take silent, private prayer seriously.

The "getting away from it all" in the experience of encountering God is also a form of protest against what caused the troubles in the first place. It enables us, with God's supportive love, to reverse the matter. It is a statement that there is more to life than what most feel is normal. Privacy is a protest against exploitation and a step toward freedom. It is in our private place that we experience God's love for us, the confirmation of our struggle toward wholeness and holiness.

What happens in the privacy of our encounter with God, apart altogether from grace and presence, is that our abilities to think, reason, imagine and be intuitive are all enhanced and used again. Like flabby muscles, they develop strength with use. God does not speak to us out of the sky but out of the powers we have been given for understanding. Inspiration, suggestion and the direction our lives should take are more easily recognized when our faculties are exercised.

In the privacy of our exchange with God, we discover that God is not a guru with an answer or a technique. God is a collaborator with us in our struggle for an authentic experience of living. God does not offer us pat answers which excuse our need to grow. We are guided forward through suggestion and intuition. That is why listening is as important as reason and common sense, why love is more important than answers. Having God solve our problems without us would belittle us. We are little enough already.

In our private exchange of love, we come to see that keeping up appearances, accepting hurtful things while resenting them, coveting attention, boasting, playing the martyr and blaming others are all phony. Christ did none of them. In the privacy of love we confront reality, our deepest reality: God. We recognize insincerities and find ourselves called beyond them. We resist, of course, because we have lived with them for so long. We have an identity which may trouble us, but it is the only identity we know. We do not know what might replace it. So we say that we cannot change. This is never a statement of fact; it is a decision to remain the way we are. In our exchange of love with God, we always arrive at a decision: to cease praying and opt for our neuroses as the easiest way out, or to allow ourselves to be loved into wholeness and health whatever the cost.

Ordinary people say that they do not know how to love God. But no technique is necessary. God's presence is personal. If we can speak to a friend, we can speak to God. As in all loving encounters, the conversation changes and develops until what matters emerges. Perhaps what matters is an aspect of our love and living which has been undervalued, leaving us impoverished. Our moments with God alert us to the truth that our loving and living have many meanings. More profound meanings are disclosed to us. It is the work of love to develop the whole person to a fuller measure of life.

We are not trapped, not even by our bodies. We are our bodies. God shatters the limited concepts we have of ourselves in the privacy of loving us. This shake-up may hurt for a bit, but it sets us free. One of our hurtful experiences is that of accepting ourselves as body and accepting the aging process. There is great freedom when we can accept our body and cherish it. People make peace with their bodies in the privacy of the bathroom. Perhaps we have never been good-looking. Or perhaps we have grown up with prominent teeth, or crossed eyes, or large ears, or too tall, too short, too flat or too big. And now we are aging. Dieting makes us slim. Exercise helps, but nothing can prevent our bodies becoming the bodies of older men and women. The lines sag; the lumps and the bulges appear; the sinews and muscles ache. In the privacy of accepting ourselves, we come to love ourselves with compassion in the totality of our being: mind, heart, feelings, flesh, birthing, nurturing and dying. What is so freeing about loving our being and becoming is that our compassion for ourselves spills over into our love for others. We can love them as God loves them, not for pretty face and figure, but in their totality of mind and heart and wrinkled flesh; in their hopes, fears, ideas and spirit; in their limits, diminishments, decline and death. This is possible because in loving God we love the Christ of God, not as mere ideal but in flesh and blood, struggle and passion and tortured death.

In the many privacies of God's love for us, we are pulled together through the passion of Christ into resurrection, into a new level of life. God knows every private depth within us. God's love is free and without condition. We are never controlled, but rather invited to share God's freedom. We are offered God's collaboration in a process of love and healing. In turn, we offer that healing to others. Ordinary people who have touched God at the center of their solitude pour out their love in deeds of compassion, caring, joy and laughter to others.

What To Do

Pupose: To discover an authentic way of loving God.

Share: Commitments to which you have been faithful.
The cost of your free decisions.
The special people you have loved.

*Background
music:*   Grieg, *Piano Conerto in A Minor Op. 16.*
Cassette tape STS5 15407.

Reflection: Center your attention on God within.
Let God be present as collaborator in your life.

End: Pray aloud Isaiah 54:4-10.

Radical Solitude

To know the solitude of one's heart is to know what is beyond all being. This is the secret wisdom of ordinary people. It is secret in that we hardly reflect on what we know. We think it unfair that we should be troubled, or lonely, or experiencing solitude. But solitude is the ground of our freedom, the possiblity or our fulfillment.

On a morning like any other, we wake up and rise. We begin the daily round routinely and without reflection. Before retiring we enter the solitude. It might be the death of a loved one, the loss of a job or a report from the doctor that what we've got is malignant. It may be something less dramatic: the midlife crisis with its depression and sense of personal mediocrity. Nothing significant has happened in our lives, we think, and nothing shall happen. It may be a daily struggle with a relationship, or our reponse to years of being victimized. Whatever it be, life is deprived of meaning. The past is so painful now that we cannot reflect on it. The future holds out no hope. There is a temptation to drown in the eternal now of the present.

We become silent, not by choice but by necessity. There simply is nothing to say. There is neither sadness nor anger, just numbness. Yet in this solitude there is something positive: the beginning of an insight into what is beyond all being, into the reality of God.

God is beyond all being. God is radical solitude. God's solitude is so radical that it originates being; it is the sourceless source, the ground of all creativity. It is the void which brings forth all that exists. It has no form; it is formative. It is not constituted; it is constitutive, the unoriginated origin, the mystery at the root of our being. We shall not know God in a mature manner until we experience that solitude ourselves.

If the solitude did not reveal its Word, we would not know that it existed. Our personal solitude would be the place of despair if it did not contain within itself the seed of some unexpected revelation, something amazingly creative. This is what enables us to persevere. Ordinary people live by hope, the hope of being originators, form-makers, creative people.

Radical solitude is too abstract a concept to engage any but the most curious of minds. It is in danger of being lost in vague statements if we fail to recognize it in the concrete realities of our lives. The God of radical solitude is found wherever people are hurting, on main street or, by way of ultimate example, in the penitentiary. When we say that someone is "in solitary," we usually mean that he or she is in an isolated cell in the penitentiary. The "pen" is the concrete example of solitude and trouble. When we enter the pen as visitors, it is not merely the solitude and functional ugliness of the buildings which strikes us, it is the carefully protected solitude of the person we are visiting. The solitude is sometimes covered up with bravado: "It's nothing. I can handle it. I'll be out of here in no time." Boastful stories about the past are told and retold, partly to shock and partly to express escapist ideas aloud. At other times the solitude is covered by an outward show of sullenness and distrust.

Troubled people act out these very same ways of coping: bravado, false optimism, silence, sullenness or boasting. It would be wrong not to respect those moods, or rather, not to respect troubled people in whatever emotional or spiritual state we find them. Nor does the theology of the troubled state call for condemnation, throwing the book at them: "Repent, brother and sister, and you will be saved." The only God that troubled people know is crucified within their own hearts. Their solitude is the solitude of

God. What troubled people most need is a friend who will bear patiently with them until some inner beauty is uncovered which might give meaning to their lives. It is a time to avoid bravado and all that is insincere, a time to search the depths of the heart where the crucified Christ is doing a healing work.

It is our emptiness which reflects the radical solitude of our Sourceless Source. Our troubled condition reveals our emergence from that Source. For that reason the Almighty "has looked upon his lowly handmaid" (Lk 1:48, *JB*). That is why God refused to deliver Paul from his weakness. Paul was too talented. God's grace was sufficient for him. That is why "despite the increase of sin, grace has far surpassed it" (Rom 5:20). For that same reason, Jesus "in the days when he was in the flesh, offered prayers and supplications with loud cries and tears to God...and he was heard because of his reverence" (Heb 5:7). This insatiable solitude of the heart is itself our experience of the divine. We are grasped by the All of God, and God expects all in return. This uncontrollable solitude sits in judgment on our desire to control things and events and condemns it. It even condemns self-control, fearful of the pride, and calls us instead to surrender ourselves to God as the Source, Meaning and Purpose of our lives.

The intuition of our roots in the radical solitide of God may also be experienced as an intense hunger for an absolute: absolute love, absolute meaning or absolute forgiveness. At other times it is felt in a moment of insight when we long for absolute beauty. It is uncovered in moments of awe or horror before unexpected good fortune or tragic loss. It has to do with all or nothing. It may be the troubled person's numbing and despairing cry for help. We realize at that moment that the solitude of God contains all that is of people, things and events; that each in its own measure shares that solitude, yet adds nothing to it since it comes forth from it. But God remains in radical solitude. Only in confronting the solitude do we come to understand that all will be well. It is possible to embrace the solitude and become co-creators with God.

When we experience hurt in our lives, it never simply stops there. It is followed by reflection in which we try to make sense of it. Perhaps it has no sense, or perhaps we impose a false sense on it. In any event this is the crucial moment. It is the moment when we decide to grow and become a new creation—a conversion experience—or we choose to be bitter and stunted. To do nothing is to regress.

Struggle With God

A young couple, Tom and Debbie, upwardly mobile, possessed of a boat, and the parents of a 2-year-old child drove out of the city to spend a day on the lake. The boat hit a submerged log and the impact hurled their child into the water. The child drowned. The police were called and the body was recovered. Debbie said that if she had been allowed to hold the child for a moment, she would have made peace with the loss. As it was, the police refused to allow the parents near the body. It was taken away for an autopsy. The parents were treated with suspicion; the impression given was that they were responsible somehow for the accident.

Their anguish led them into a deep solitude. They might have become bitter. They did not because their faith sustained them. They understood enough to know that anger with God or with the police is largely self-indulgent. They got through the process of mourning. It taught them that absence is not non-existence, though they wept for grief.

When the process was over and they had made peace with the solitude, they received a gift of the Spirit which enriched their lives. It made them recall the words of Jesus: "Unless I go, the Advocate will not come to you" (Jn 16:7). Had they not accepted the loss, the gift would not have been given to them. Their gift was a grace and a decision. Out of the solitude they went on a mission of mercy to all other grieving parents. Whenever they hear of the death of a child, they go to the grieving parents to assist and console them. They have made this their ministry. Out of the radical solitude comes the creative word, the gift of the Spirit.

Struggle with loss is struggle with God. The whole purpose is that troubled people should come to the depths of their inner silence. Inner silence is an open door to the experience of God. It is God, of course, who is the seeker. But our minds and hearts are full of the world's noise. This erects a barrier. God struggles to communicate something of lasting worth, but communication is difficult. It takes a traumatic struggle to tear down our barriers. By way of example: When we try to comunicate with a deaf person or with someone whose language we do not speak, there is a struggle. Only rarely is there clear understanding. But in the struggle we are formed anew and the results are worth the concentrated effort. It is in this manner that God struggles with us. Out of the solitude in the struggle comes understanding. It is not a matter of information, but the realization of how deeply we are united and how great is our love. God was there all the time and the unity was intact. The mind, previously distracted by sense impressions, upward mobility, now experiences a higher level of awareness, a true unity with the mystery. We now know what it is that we should be doing.

We were complacent. Now we know that what is grasped by the senses is not the whole of reality. But the radical solitude which brings the whole of reality into being may be experienced in any one aspect of being: in a tragic loss, a gentle breeze, a place, an emotion, a moment of friendship, a burning bush, an experience of beauty. It is in such a moment of silence that we come to the intuition of our depths within the solitude of God. It is then that we are chosen by the Word and sent on our way to proclaim the goodness and purpose of our existence. Out of the silence and solitude comes something creative for others, rarely for ourselves—though it gives purpose to our lives.

The greatness of Tom and Debbie, of a Dorothy Day, a Martin Luther King, a Mozart, a Mahler or a Van Gogh is not in who they were in themselves but in who they were for other people. Digging up their past and finding flaws of character there, even sin, does not diminish who they were in God's scheme of things. Their personal lives of loss, poverty, psychosis, alcoholism, emotional insecurity or regretted sinfulness was the radical solitude of God. Contrast their lives with that of the millionaire art collector with his electric fences and guard dogs, or with the pietistic holy man or vote-conscious politician. They have nothing to offer others because their concern is with their own pseudo-salvation. An Islamic mystic, Abu Yazid, put it well:

The Gnostic is concerned with what he knows and with his hopes;
the ascetic with what he eats. Blessed is he who is concerned with

one thing only and whose heart is not distracted.... . You, Lord,
are the object of my desire.

There is a God for the troubled who long for God. There is no God but
only an idol for the complacent who think they comprehend God. The radical solitude of the divine remains just that, incomprehensible. It is revealed
in that God continues to be absolute mystery. The mystery is, in fact, inconceivable in itself. It is inconceivable not in the sense that what is not
now known will later be understood, but in the strictest sense that God is
incomprehensible for human minds. The solitude remains intact. God
dwells in "inaccessible light." That is why troubled people experience pain
and loss. In our problems we come to know and endure the otherness of
God and the mystery, as indeed God must also endure our otherness. It is
in this solitude itself that we experience God.

Certainly God speaks. The Word "leaps down" in silences which set
people free to do the works of mercy for others. But the works and the
words are mostly ours, and they need to be tested. Getting high on Jesus
can be an evasion, no more holy than getting high on one of our addictions.
In the final analysis we are called:

Only to do the right and to love goodness, and to walk humbly
with your God (Mi 6:8).

We surrender our egotism to the solitude, allowing the divinity its reality,
it allowing us ours.

Were there no struggle, neither solitude nor tension in our lives, we
would quickly become bored. We need the unforseen. People whose actions and words are predictable usually tire us. It is the incomprehensible
which excites us. Unpredictable and incomprehensible people, "charac-
ters" we call them because they have character, hold our attention. They
also try our patience. Could one expect less of God? It is the very mystery
of God which will be the source of our eternal and ecstatic joy... limitless
surprises, never knowing when the rabbit will pop out of the hat. The mystery of radical solitude, experienced in the traumas of life, does not narrow
the horizon of our lives but expands it. The further we journey into God,

the greater the mystery will be, the deeper the joy. Should such a journey end, God would only be finite.

> *The end of the worship of God is that he who worships should pass away in worship, and be lost in the One whom he worships...and this is the state in which perishability perishes, fana al-fana* (The Sufi Mystic Jani in *Nafahat al-Uns*).

"In the Middle of Nowhere"

Our longing for God, the source of all our discontent, will never be satisfied until we confront and accept our solitude. In the most mundane events of our lives we are surrounded by mystery and must die into it.

There is a figure of speech called an "Irish Bull." It is a statement inconsistent with itself; it contains a logical contradiction. Webster defines it as "an incongruous statement." One has the feeling that Webster is voicing a common enough prejudice which holds that all statements should have a precise and logical meaning. Statements which have a precise meaning, despite their pragmatic value, are dead statements. Words which have but one precise meaning are dead words. A life, precise and ordered, under control but without mystery, is a living death. Statements, words and life should lead beyond themselves and open us out to the mystery of existence. That is what the Irish bull is trying to do.

The Irish define this figure of speech by using it: "An Irish Bull is pregnant with meaning," they say. Tourists, American mostly, come away from the pubs speaking of how cute the forms of expression used by the natives are. They attribute it to a mixture of mysticism and whiskey. The "Mysticism of the Gael" is a crock of stuff invented by the emigrants, and whiskey rarely turns prose into poetry. It is a matter of intuition. There are experiences which transcend logic and reason, experiences which have nothing dead about them. They cannot be grasped or expressed in rational statements. And the incongruous is not cute; it is very seriously trying to cope with the experience of mystery. Still less is it "bull" in the American sense of the word.

There is a story containing an Irish bull which goes like this:

• *An American rent-a-car tourist made a wrong turn and got lost in the middle of an Irish bog. He chanced on a turf-cutter, stopped and got out of the car.*

• *"Shure, 'tis lost in the middle of nowhere you are, isn't it?" said the turf-cutter.*

• *"It is indeed, sir," said the tourist. "I wonder if you might tell me how I can get from here to Donegal?"*

• *"Well then, if 'tis going to Donegal you are," replied the sage, "you wouldn't start from here at all..."*

• *The tourist smiled.*

• *"...Go back now to the village. When you get there, follow your nose up the hill an' 'twill surely get you to Donegal."*

The logical contradiction is contained in the statement, "you wouldn't start from here at all." *Here*, where he is lost, is the middle of nowhere. The question is not whether the tourist ever got to Donegal. What must be asked is how the turf-cutter found himself in the middle of nowhere. That he was aware of that center and accepting of it argues toward his having found himself.

Let us bring this pregnant bull to labor.

"Lost in the middle of nowhere" is a symbol of radical solitude, in fact, a symbol of infinity. Finding ourselves there is an experience of union of God. There is no possible way in which we can go from the middle of nowhere to somewhere. This center has no definable point; it is everywhere. The measure of the finite, on the other hand, reaches from one precise point to another, point A to point B. It is logical, rational and precise; for example, a journey from the village to Donegal. If our only journey in life is concerned with the finite, we shall surely arrive there. But life's meaning, which is a search for the infinite, will be lost.

When we want to get away from it all, to go on vacation, it is evidence enough that we long for God, though many may not be aware of that. Ordinary people hunger for God in very ordinary ways, ways not always connected with religion. Longing for God is a call which summons us to drop everything and head for the wide-open spaces, the hills or the ocean, the middle of nowhere. Vacationers hear the call and respond. More theologically put, the Word of God leads us back to the radical solitude: "No one comes to the Father but through me" (Jn 14:6).

The bog, the ocean, the lake, the hills or the middle of nowhere are not God—that would be pantheism. But for a short moment God is discovered in the wide-open spaces, which is something altogether different. The whole of reality may be revealed in any one of its theophanies: "eternity in a grain of sand." The turf-cutter was not interested in getting to Donegal because he had found himself where an open door to God was revealed. It was a matter of experience transcending reason, mystery being more than logic. Whether or not the family heading for the hills or the ocean recognizes this open door in the middle of nowhere depends on how they accept their time "away from it all." They may never reflect on it, but they are finding the Ground of their being in that out-of-the-way place. The troubled person, lost in the middle of nowhere, is experiencing the solitude of God.

The solitude may be experienced anywhere, not merely in church. It may be found in loneliness or emotional need, in the heart of a poor person or a child, in the hills, the ocean or the bog. Out of the experience of the center of infinity come the forms of religion. Forms are constructed to cope with the mystery. Through symbol and story we re-form our world to prevent our going mad. But if there is no mystery, our reformations are empty. The forms are merely secondary.

Putting Forms on the Solitude

We are not part of anyone else. When, as ordinary people, we look within our hearts, we know we stand alone in our nowhereness. No one else may plumb that depth within us. It is the holy place. It is within that solitude that we become persons. It is here that we are unique, standing over against other unique persons, offering them our deliberate love. This is the manner in which we create our forms, the forms of religion and culture. We bring forth our "word" within the Word of God. This is the fruit of our spirit which reveals to others who we are. A person, a culture or a religion devoid of the fruits of the human spirit—music, art, literature, architecture, painting, as well as liturgy and self-transcendence—is devoid of God, however loudly one proclaims, "Lord, Lord." We give witness to the reality of God not only through prayer, worship and proclamation but through creative works and acts of service to others. These are the forms which ordinary people are summoned to create lest they drown in self-pity and the infinite. It is in the creative act that we experience the solitude we call "Father."

We create forms only from what we experience personally and first-hand. Everything else is longed-for. It is not sufficient to live our lives in endless longing. We need to make the divine real.

> Not that anybody has seen the Father,
> except the one who comes from God:
> he has seen the Father (Jn 6:46, *JB*).

Only the Word which the solitude has spoken can reveal our origin to us. Only the Word can lead us back to the source. It is only when we abandon ourselves to Christ and accept his way of self-emptying as our way also that we arrive at the radical solitude, the creative source or our reformation. We do not lay greedy hands on that source—our capacity is too limited and confused. This is a way of saying that God is not the object of logic, magic or charm. The solitude is not a specimen to be examined by science. God is attained, not grasped, by our dying into God, a maturing experience brought about by the challenges of life. The solitude is known in faith for what it is when we entrust ourselves to it. It purifies us and gives us joy. It establishes community and communion.

There is a decrease of egotism in people who have experienced and accepted life's troubles. There is no ego at all in God. The solitude gives all it is to the Word, nothing remains. "Just as all that belongs to me is yours, so all that belongs to you is mine" (Jn 17:10). There is no ego. The medium of the troubled person's encounter with God is no egotistical stance but an intuition, a contemplative gaze on the middle of nowhere. Whatever be the encounter of others, that of a person in trouble is at the heart of the mystery. It is in that solitude that we are formed into the image and like-ness of God. It is there that we receive power to re-form, in our own small but unique way, the world about us. This is the secret of Augustine, Fran-cis of Assisi, Bach, Beethoven, Martin Luther King, Mother Teresa and of all others who have died into the mystery at the center of their being.

What we do with the center of nowhere, the experienced solitude, deter-mines who we shall be in the world which nurtures us. The losses, disap-pointments, betrayals and depressions are evaluated in the context of God in such a way that they dissipate our egotism. They open us to new forms of creative living, new forms of work and art, of service to others and last-ing friendships. They put meat on the dry bones of liturgy. The losses, betrayals and disappointments become poetry, music, insight, ministry, prayer, worship and theology.

All troubled people know God in their solitude, even when at times they are unable to put that knowledge into concept and forms. It is beyond con-cept. This is the experience of God which is sensed as the "divine dark-ness" of the pseudo-Dionysius, the *"nada"* of John of the Cross, the "emptiness and void" of Meister Eckhart or of *The Cloud of Unknowing*. Yet, that dark knowing is something positive, formative and fulfilling. It is the only knowing that will ultimately satisfy a person's longing for in-finity.

Van Gogh, being merely human, went mad slowly, driven deep into his radical solitude. Out of it came the paintings which amaze the world. Mozart died in poverty and neglect. Out of him came the music which heals our hearts. Beethoven went deaf and never heard his *Ode to Joy*. Out of our personal agony comes our creative word.

God is an artist. Out of God's solitude came the masterpiece of the universe, the Word made flesh. We also incarnate our solitude in the new person we become, in our new form, that we may be one of God's master-pieces. It is done in silence, a process of change, not a program anyone can offer us. The Word enfleshed, which is the world's art, reveals the Mystery to us:

"The word you hear is not mine;
it comes from the Father who sent me" (Jn 4:24).

To recognize our word within the Word of God is to have a moment of illumination which comes from contact with the mind of God. It is a gift. And yet, even if our minds are closed and our eyes blinded by the dust of our world, our longing, any longing, reveals our need for the One who alone can satisfy the human heart. The solitude invades us, welcomed or not. It sends us forth to create forms of understanding, to proclaim the Word.

In the beginning was Kmvoum; today is Kmvoum;
tomorrow will be Kmvoum.
Who can make an image of Kmvoum, he has no body.
He is a word that comes out of your mouth.
That word. It is no more;
it is past and it still lives!
So is Kmvoum (A prayer from the Pygmies of Zaire).

What To Do

Purpose: To confront the Mystery of God.

Share: What the isolating experiences of your life have been.
What events made you feel alone.
What you learned from loneliness.

Background music: Dvorak, *Cello Concerto in B Minor, Op. 104*
on cassette tape Quintessence P4C-7142.

Quiet time: Reflect on your solitude being the solitude of God.
Your inner silence is an open invitation to God.
Your creativity is who you are for other people.

End: Pray aloud Psalm 66.

The Mirror Image

The Word

God made the world to discover who God is.

One could conceive of the God of radical solitude looking into the mirror of its mind and having a pure God-thought. It would be pure intelligibility, infinite, beyond all structure, without highlights or contrasts. It would be so pure and limitless that, as far as we are concerned, it would be nothing. The solitude would be nothing if it did not give expression to itself and originate something. That something is its Word.

A voice cries out:
in the desert prepare the way of the Lord (Is 40:3).

This is the coming of the Beloved. "This Son is the reflection of the Father's glory, the exact representation of the Father's being, and he sustains all things by his powerful word" (Heb 1:3). What the creative solitude saw when it looked into the mirror of its wise and loving mind was its "self," the mirror image reflecting all that God is.

When we speak of one person of the Trinity, the Creative solitude, we must at the same time be conscious of its Word and their Spirit. Not to do so would be to distort the Mystery. Such a contemplative and comprehensive gaze on the Trinity is, of course, desirable; it is not easily attainable. So we speak of one person at a time while not forgetting the other two. In the beginning was the Word;

> the Word was in God's presence,
> and the Word was God (Jn 1:1).

The Word, from the beginning, is all the radical solitude is: "Whoever has seen me has seen the Father" (Jn 14:9).

Everything has a word, be it a barn, a house, a tree or any ordinary person. It is the inner essence of what a thing, a person or an event is. The word is revelation. It will proclaim the truth or dishonesty of what is observed. A well-crafted and functional barn has more honesty, a truer word, than an expensive mansion built to the vanity and bad taste of its owner. The building tells us who the builder is. Music was W.C. Handy's word; "The St. Louis Blues" tells us something of the spirituality of the composer. Song is the singer's word. Paintings proclaim the inspiration of the painter. What makes us laugh exposes the goodness or evil or our souls. But things made to deceive us, plastic flowers or fake furs, are false words. That they sometimes cost more than the real article is no redeeming feature.

The presence of the Word is most powerfully experienced where we find love and allow ourselves to be loved. Primarily this is in other people. But it is also discovered within ourselves when we accept our environment in the world. Our environment is a home, a habitat for life. It nurtures love, life and joy. Troubled people must search for a home in the world. We can isolate ourselves from the people within our environment, not allowing them to touch our minds and hearts. We do this when we take everything for granted, filtering out all we consider irrelevant, the things which do not seem to feed our self-interest. Then we become sad. It is the absence of the Word.

To recognize the Word, we must not consider anything irrelevant. We need to pay attention. To have joy in the Word, we must never cease to search for joy. The Word is not a possession. It is common to all. Those things which are not possessed but belong to everyone heal us and bring the purest joy. Possessions bring anxiety and the fear of loss. Pure joy is possible when there is no possessiveness or fear of loss. Within the Word in whom all lesser words exist we bring forth the word of the seemingly irrelevant in our environment with joy. It might be the sight of the mountains, the beauty of what remains of the prairies in the variety of wild flowers and grasses by the roadside, the smell of mint and hay on a summer morning, the rumble of trains through the valley, the sound of traffic. Paying attention with love to the environment expands our heart with joy. It is the birthing of the word. They are all words within the Word of God, and they bring us home to our true self. They are the environment of our home on the planet where people are loved with conscious will. The lakes, mountains, pine-covered hills and even the most pathetic of people open our heart to the Word once we see that they are our home.

Everything that is good, true and beautiful is charged with grace, the power and presence of God. Every word of the Word is a theophany, a shining forth of the glory of God. This is possible because the Word reveals God's inner essence made flesh and making its home among us. Through, in and for the Word everything was made and "apart from him nothing came to be" (Jn 1:3). God's joy is ours. Now "your joy can be complete" (Jn 15:11).

But something happened which is at the root of all our troubles. We fail to hear the Speaker in the Word, in any word. Our sight is dimmed, and what we do see does not always bring joy.

Adam Fell in Sumpter, Oregon

When God looked into the mirror of solitude, he saw not only the Word but every other word as well. The solitude came to know its "self." With all the simplicity of divine innocence, God saw that it was very good indeed (Gn 1:31). All words, in lesser or greater fashion, imaged the divine. There would be risk in allowing freedom to one of the created species. Yet without their being free, God would be at best the owner of a toy factory. How tiresome toys would become—mere images without likeness. God risked the rebellion inherent in freedom, and the mirror shattered into many million fragments. It was not at all that it ceased to be good, but that in the multiplicity of splinters it became difficult to see God's self anymore. The people would have eyes and not see, ears and not hear, yet remain, fundamentally, very good indeed.

Humankind as a whole, under the generic term Adam, understood itself to be called by God to name things, give them their word, bring forth their inner essence. "The LORD God...brought them to the man to see what he would call them; whatever the man called each of them would be its name" (Gn 2:19). It is Adam's privilege to know the word of each thing. In knowing their real essence as word within the Word, Adam will see God revealed in them. Through what is made we know the maker. As great composers are known in their music, so God is known as a wise and loving God in all created things. The divine is known as a God for others, a caring God. It was this clear vision which Adam lost. We fail to see the Word because we see and taste a forbidden word.

What Adam chose to see, and still sees, was how things could be coveted, used and manipulated for personal purposes, for power, greed and pleasure. The eyes of his perception became blinded, the doors of his consciousness closed.

The original sin which Adam transmits to us is not a substance or an act. One's acts, sinful or otherwise, cannot be handed on to others. We hand our blindness on to others, pass it down to our children, a new distorted word, a false revelation which contains a very seductive experience: the gain, power and pleasure that may be had when we use the world as an end in itself. We are denied the word of God and we pay the price in our many troubles.

On Labor Day of last year I went with two friends, Margie and Betty, to Sumpter, Oregon. Sumpter is a ghost-town, an old abandoned mining center. We had no more purpose than God has when he was "moving about the garden at the breezy time of the day" (Gn 3:8).

To our surprise, things seemed well in Sumpter. It was celebrating. There was a carnival atmosphere. Booths were set up on every street; they spilled over into the fields. People had come in campers from all over the Northwest to sell "antiques." It seemed that every turn-of-the-century home had been ransacked for cheap bric-a-brac: porcelain dogs, blue and red glass vases, tea sets, old brown photographs, basins and ewers, coffee grinders. There was laughter, music, bunting and all the cherished words of another time and culture. Paradise was spread out before us. One man had a sign over his booth which read: "Junque." And Eve was there.

Eve wanted Adam, who had care of a booth and had dominion over it, to do what it was his privilege to do: name a certain object, call forth its inner essence, give it its word.

"Is it," she enquired, pointing to the object on the grass, "a soup tureen or a chamberpot?"

Had this not been the universal woman, but a mere Northwesterner, she would have named it a thunder-mug, as do people in these parts.

Adam failed the test, and fell in Sumpter, Oregon. Not that he told a lie. He refused to call forth the word in sincerity and truth. His vision was distorted by his desire to make a profit. He erased from his mind the real need of the woman and any thought of the trouble he could have caused her. It was his deviousness, not profit-making, which was his downfall. As a pragmatist, he well knew how to manipulate the world. He avoided the question. He lost clear vision.

"Nowadays," he replied, "people often grow flowers in them."

She refused the evasion. This humble piece of crockery was mystery awaiting revelation.

"Yes, but is it a soup tureen or a chamber pot?" she persisted.

Adam changed his tactics. Like a TV preacher he proceeded to reduce what was essentially a religious and revelatory moment to mere ethics.

"There would be nothing wrong in using it as a soup tureen," he replied. It was a fascinating moment. I could not help but wonder what her husband would say on being presented with his soup. True enough, there would not have been anything morally wrong with eating one's soup from a thunder-mug. But it would violate the word, the inner being of this faithful servant of humanity. The pot deserved a better fate. Things, events and people are honored by respecting who and what they are in their inner being.

Eve mused for a while and then wandered off murmuring: "But it does not have a lid."

We rounded a corner and there on the grass was one with a lid. I cried out, "Hell, Margie, here's a piss-pot with a lid on it." (They were so designated in the Ireland of my youth.) People looked up. "There was silence," as it were, "in heaven" for about half an hour (Rv 8:1).

We had just been present at original sin.

What Adam passes on to us daily is the blindness which comes from self-interest. To find the Mystery of God revealed to us in the daily word calls for a cleansing of our eyes and an opening of the doors of our consciousness. Should we fail in this endeavor, our troubles will overwhelm us. Whether we be as lowly as a thunder-mug or as high as the sky, the solution to our troubles lies before our eyes in the "word" that is spoked to us.

What the world needed was a New Adam, a Word containing within itself every word. It needed a word which could restore to one the splintered pieces of the mirror. Out of the solitude this word became flesh

and we have seen his glory;
The glory of an only Son coming from the Father (Jn 1:14).

Now, the solitude knows its self. When we name things correctly, that is in the power and presence of Christ's Spirit, we restore the broken' image of God in the world. We heal the problem. The world's people and its events reveal God to those who have clear vision. "Blest are the single-hearted for they shall see God" (Mt 5:8), today and every day. And when we uncover the solitude of God imaged in our own troubled state, we also reveal the mystery of God to Itself. God and the world are mutually relieving each other's ignorance.

When our human species arrived at self-determination and knew the possibility of opting for ourselves alone, uncaring of the whole, we became divided from our Source. Dualism entered our world. Unity and singleness of purpose were lost. We fell from instinct into culture, from contemplation into crass commercialism. We discovered the loss of things and the resulting fear. We invented weapons to protect ourselves from the loss. We became divided from the world about us. We now look on it with the cold uncomprehending eyes of strangers. We ask how we might use it, covet it, consume it and fight for it. This is sin, and trouble enough for all of us. The missiles are merely sin's incarnation.

It is still possible to discover the deeper meaning. We may create a space within, a receptiveness for the Word, a sort of question mark in the back of our minds which asks of every event what it is that God is revealing. Troubled people, more than others, are led to those questions. It is not that any given sense experience, any given trouble, need be extraordinary. Retaining the prosaicness of mediocrity, our troubles reveal a more profound truth and call us to action. It is in this intuitive moment that we come to know God personally and intimately. This is knowing the divine rather than knowing about it. The problems and rituals which bring us to this knowing are not ends in themselves; their purpose is to lead us further on our journey into God.

Clear vision—seeing something and experiencing its deeper meaning as word and revelation—is always attested to in the lives of people of prayer. Such people are less apt to be tainted by the dualism which colored the waters of Christianity to no good purpose: matter versus spirit, inner versus outer, earth versus heaven. Both matter and spirit are created by God. They are of equal importance. The grace of God in power and presence is not revealed in spirit alone. It is manifest in a deer leaping across a meadow, in the flight of an eagle, in the flow of water. It is, of course, present in a more profound manner in the life of a loving person. All living and inanimate things are words within the Word of God for those who have cleansed their eyes.

The Celtic church was spared the dualism of the Greeks for several centuries. One of its most notable features is clear vision. "The power of the Lord is in the paw of the cat," a young Celtic monk cried when his cat caught a salmon wallowing in the shallows. The chronicles tell of the *peregrini,* the wandering sailor monks of the Atlantic, seeing the angels of God and hearing their song as they rose and fell over the western is- lands. To the scientific man they were only gulls and gannets, puffins, cormorants and kittiwakes. But the monks lived in a world in which everything was a word of God to them, in which the power of God was manifest to anyone with the least creative imagination. How else, they wondered, would God speak to them. They cherished the scriptures, but they also cherished God's ongoing revelation in their lives. "Nature breaks through the eyes of a cat," they said. But that nature was a theophany. For the eyes of faith, all events, troubled or pleasant, contain the power and providence of God. There is a Creed attributed to St. Patrick which is no dry intellectual formula. It sees the Word of God's revelation in the whole of nature, not merely in intellectual abstractions:

> God of heaven and earth and every star;
> of mountain high and valley low,
> —God dwells in all things that are

in heaven and earth and sea below.
He breathes life in them, he gives them light,
He makes the sun shine bright.
He is over all; he is under all.
He forms wells in dry earth; dry islands in the sea.
    he has a Son as old as he,
and the Spirit is their breath.
        Not separate
are Father, Son and Spirit, three.

No word is a last word, not even a *symbolum fidei,* a symbol of faith, a creed. Everything, even our troubles, symbolizes something deeper. Our whole experience of life must lead beyond itself into the depths of God.

Words and Wonder

In a culture in which we feel that ultimately science and technology will answer all problems, we have lost much of our sense of the sacred. This results in our not being able to see the Word of God speaking to us out of our ordinary experiences. Nor are the "holy place," the "sacred moment" or the sanctifying event the commonplaces of everyday experience. They are relegated to dry ritual events performed, rather than celebrated, on Sunday mornings. What the troubled person is learning is that healing and forgiveness, chronic illness and bereavement must be celebrated in our secular world before they can be meaningfully celebrated in community rituals. Our troubles are not a call to isolation but a summons to service. A phone call, a get-well card, a visit are the basic ingredients of life which enable us to survive. They precede our celebrations of reconciliation, anointings, imposing of hands. We ordinary people are called to break bread with others before ever we break it in church. We must come out of our isolation.

We search for a spiritual understanding of our troubled state. It is not ideas but experiences that are our concern. Ideas are always from the past. Philosophers are interested in ideas, scientists in the functioning of things. A religious person is interested in the inner understanding of an event. God did not make revelation, express his Word, in ideas but in mighty and not so mighty deeds. As scripture points out so often, it is inner understanding that we need: "Know, and fix in your heart that the Lord is God in the heavens above and on earth below, and that there is no other" (Dt 4:39). Also, "It is love that I desire, not sacrifice, and knowledge of God (in Jewish terms: intimate personal experience) rather than holocausts" (Hos 6:6). And again: "The Lord spoke to you from the midst of the fire. You heard the sound of the words, but saw no form; there was only a voice" (Dt 4:12). God speaks to us through the medium of our pain and troubles. They are God's voice calling us to growth and creativity. No form of the divinity is visible. The forms in which we express our understanding are our own.

Our way to the discovery of God in the troubled condition is one of wondering, an openness to the mystery of reality. "Reality lies beyond my grasp; and deep, so deep, who can discover it?" (Eccl 7:24, *JB*). A troubled spirit may hear the Word of God in something as simple as a sunset. We see the glory of God which transcends the heavens. The whole of Psalm 113 is a prayer of a person in trouble. This moment of beauty calls us beyond the limitations of the earth to freedom. We experience a hunger which God alone can satisfy. We experience God's healing and delivering presence. We wondered ourselves into it.

What makes us wonder is the sublime, a threshold *(limina)* experience. Even tragedy can be sublime in the original sense of that which inspires awe. We do not look at the threshold but across it to the world beyond. The door opens in our heart and we look beyond it to God. The sublime triggers our capacity for mystery. Our intuition that there is more to life than we have been experiencing is not some new idea. It is a longing for healing which can only be found in God. The sublime means nothing to cattle. Even humans need to be sensitized to it. The scriptures never celebrate the charm or beauty of nature—something self-indulgent; they celebrate the grandeur and sublimity of life.

Every trouble we have is sublime because it is a share in the passion of the Word. It evokes humility:

> "My being proclaims the greatness of the Lord,
> my spirit finds joy in God my savior,
> For he has looked upon his servant in her lowliness" (Lk 1:46-48).

Without humility, the most sublime moment or event will be sheer nonsense; reverence is wanting.

> The reason why the adult no longer wonders is not because he has solved the riddle of existence, but because he has become accustomed to the laws governing his world...he has lost the art of reflective thinking (Max Planck).

Anselm of Canterbury mourned: "The senses of my soul have grown rigid and dull, obstructed by long listlessness." Even Anselm could be spiritually and mentally lazy. Troubled people need a radical amazement toward all of reality because the wonder of being is an important part of our religious heritage. It is an important ingredient in our inner healing.

Without wonder, knowledge makes us conceited and dull, or it makes us shrewd, teaching us how to use others. Wonder consecrates us to the Word, setting us aside as sacred to God. We begin to see the world as God sees it. When we arrive at seeing the world and all its events within the Word of God—they are there because of creation and incarnation—we begin to sense the transformation of the world into the reign of God. We recover the sense of the sacred, of the holy place and moment. We see the glory.

The glory is present: "All of us, gazing on the Lord's glory with unveiled faces, are being transformed from glory to glory into his very image by the Lord who is the Spirit" (2 Cor 3:18). The glory of God has always filled the whole world. This glory reveals God's presence. It is the radiance which enables people to see the Word. It is the shining forth of the God who dwells in inaccessible light. The glory is God, hidden and revealed. A person's talent might bring out the inner glory of that person—a Dorothy Day, a Jackson Pollock, a Woody Guthrie—but the person remains a mystery. The glory of God shines on the crucified face of Christ. It is revealed as a Word. Ordinary people gaze on that face and wonder at that beauty, that they also may share the glory.

For God, who said, "Let light shine out of darkness,"
has shone in our hearts, that we in turn might make known
the glory of God shining on the face of Christ (2 Cor 4:6).

What To Do

Purpose: To find yourself within the Word of God.

Input: Everything has a "word." Everything makes a statement: people, cars, houses, dogs, cats and especially, God.

Background music: *The Baroque Harp,* Vox CT 2262.

Quiet time: Reflect on your word, what statement you wish to make to others by the way you live your life.

Sharing: What statement God makes to you through the beauty of nature.
What you know of God by knowing Jesus of Nazareth. What word of God you would wish to be to others.

End: Pray aloud Psalm 8.

The Genius Of God

Gifts

Some things we save, some things we discard. Those we discard become garbage and are hauled off to the dump. That is because what is merely functional gets used up and thrown away. Mere functionaries go to hell—so to speak. The things we save are not necessarily our most expensive possessions. They may have very little financial or artistic value, or none at all. We save cheap souvenirs from trips we've made, old photographs, gifts from special people, perhaps a special letter.

They are saved because they have spirit. They did not always have spirit. It is something they received. They received the spirit through a relationship with someone or something other than themselves. What is merely functional has no spirit; it is there to be used up. What has spirit is saved because spirit can never be used up. Things and people with spirit are sacraments, sacred signs. They have a gospel, a good news story to tell. They are a memorial; they recall an event out of the past into the present. They establish communion.

It is not possible to define spirit. It is not an object. It is the real genius of a thing. The genius of a person may be revealed in that person's work, but what genius is itself is a mystery. It is possible to experience it and recognize its presence, but it is not something "out there." It is a power which reveals the incomprehensible, yet a power which is not subject to scientific measurement. It opens us to the mystery of being.

We have to have some form of intimacy or personal involvement with a thing, a person or an event to recognize the spirit there. It is not there to entertain us but to expand our own spirit. A philistine will stand before a Monet painting and pick his nose; a person who understands what Monet experienced when he painted will stand there holding back tears. Franco Zifferelli wrote of Maria Callas: "I firmly believe that she was an instrument of God to teach us beauty throught her singing, and so make us better people." All great art has been touched by the Spirit of God, as has all great prayer. We should approach both not to discover whether we like it or not, but to experience what its creator experienced when moved by God to bring it forth. There we come to know that the spirit is a creative love. In that moment we become creators ourselves as we discover our own genius for love and creativity.

Many ordinary people have little exposure to great art. What we all have in common in the area of intuitive genius is the opportunity to give a gift. A gift without spirit is a payoff, an obligation, a bribe or some other such abomination. It is a violation of the human person. God is gift, self-gift. The genius of God's self-gift is the Holy Spirit. God's gift is neither bribe nor payoff.

When we decide to buy a gift for someone—a child, for example—we go to the store, and there on the shelf are hundreds of stuffed-with-sawdust toys. They have neither spirit, story nor personality. They are not yet communion. We see one that is apt because it says what we wish to say to the child about our love, because it will be acceptable to the child and understood. We pick it out and buy it, and immediately it becomes the bearer of our love and our spirit to our young friend. The child will receive it and cherish, not in the context of what it cost, not even in the context of its artistic value, but in the awareness of our love and thoughtfulness. Now we have established a communion of mind and spirit with our friend. "You are a genius," she will say. "You gave me the gift I most cherish." The toy is now vastly more than its stuffed-with-sawdust self. It now has a story of good news; it has established communion; it is saved as a memorial. It has spirit. In a sense it is eucharist, a thanksgiving memorial of an unselfish deed. Adults give gifts to each other, sometimes apt, sometimes not. We all need to be gifted so as to be saved from our mere sawdust self, our ordinary condition.

Christ came as gift from the Father to save us from the damage. He bore, bared and brought forth the Spirit of the Father which was his Spirit also. He came as a gift, wrapped with the Spirit, to be received by us with joy, "that my joy may be yours," he said, "and your joy may be complete" (Jn 15:11). It was the Genius of God which made Christ the apt gift. It is the same Genius/Spirit which enables us to recognize the gift and accept it. Giver and gift are one. We accept the gift, and accepting it receive the Spirit of the Father. The Spirit in which the gift was given becomes ours.

In Christ we are inspirited. The stuffed-with-sawdust self of ordinary people matters not at all. We are not saved because of our sawdust self but because of the Spirit which rests on us. We are ourselves gift to the Father, bearing Christ's Spirit. We have a story to tell. It has to do with the ways we were chosen, the troubles we endured and the communion we have with the Giver and the Gift. Our story is part of the ongoing gospel which is written until the whole body, head and members, enters the kingdom. It began with Jesus of Nazareth:

"My word is not my own:...
the Holy Spirit,
whom the Father will send in my name,
will teach you everything" (Jn 14:24-26, *JB*).

God chose Jesus as self-gift. God's spirit rested on him: "This is my Son, my Chosen One. Listen to him" (Lk 9:35). We who have accepted him share in his being as gift. We are called beyond our sawdust limitations and failures. Our purpose in life is not so much to succeed as to accept God in pure gift. This is the meaning of who we are. "You must know that your body is a temple of the Holy Spirit, who is within—the Spirit you have received from God" (1 Cor. 6:19).

God is a Maker. The Art of God is the fruit of God's Genius. We are all called to be co-creators by sharing that Genius. We create our own being in, with and through the power of God's Genius. It is in this power that we pray (Rom 8). The troubled person has to be concerned with the Giver and the Gift, not with the frail self which accepts it. We have to be empty of any conniving self so as to be open to the gift.

By the restless drive for success we become a "somebody" and cling to this somebody who exists only in the mirrored reflection in the eyes of our admirers. In prayer this somebody must die so that we be liberated to receive our true glory and true fulfullment from the hands of God (James Finley, *Merton's Palace of Nowhere*).

What the Spirit accomplishes through the gift is at times communication: The Spirit will instruct you in everything, and remind you of all that I told you" (Jn 14:26). At other times the gift is silent, not informing us of anything. It is there to bring us back to our Source. Just as we have union with a person to whom we gave a gift, so have we union with God by accepting the Son in the power and presence of the Spirit. The purpose of God's union with us is more than Gospel story: It is communion of mind and heart. God's self-gift is accepted with gratitude. In return, we make the gift of ourselves to God, and God gives thanks (*eucharistein*). This is communion with the Genius of God in Christ.

Pobrecita

Juanita had worked in the fields throughout the whole of her life. She did stoop labor to support Papá and the kids. Papá was a "simple" man, ashamed to be seen in church. Juanita was tired, a spiritless woman with lines of exhaustion in her face. She never smiled. When she came to church on Sunday mornings, to the Spanish Mass, I always put my arm round her shoulders and gave her a hug in a vain effort to get her to smile. She had stopped smiling.

One afternoon she was rummaging through some cartons of old clothing in the church basement. She had all the expectancy and helplessness of the very poor.

"Could I have these?" she asked, looking up from the rummage and holding a pair of bright brown shoes. "Papá could use them."

"Oh sure, sure! Anything you want."

The following Sunday, after the English Liturgy, I was surprised to see Juanita coming out of church with Papá hanging on her arm. He was wearing the bright shoes, and Juanita was smiling. For one bright moment, I saw God wearing the Universe.

Papá with the great courtesy of his people, had come to give thanks. He thought it fitting, Juanita explained, that he should come to the larger congregation at the English Liturgy. But it was we who received from him.

It was his moment of communion. The need to give thanks (eucharist) summed up what his life was all about. The symbol this time was not bread and wine but shoes. Out of the solitude of the very poor comes the creative act, and God walked out of church wearing bright brown shoes. Now, Papá comes every Sunday and Juanita smiles a lot.

In himself alone Van Gogh was no more than the leftovers of his art. He created from the depths of his psychosis. Mozart, drunk and a debtor, was squeezed dry by his genius. Merton remained an emotional adolescent to the end, struggling to make sense of his world. Therese of Lisieux went through a severe neurotic period. People of genius are wrung out. It was the Genius of God which squeezed Jesus dry and hung him up for the sake of the covenant in his blood. The Genius of God crucifies the ego of all who accept the incarnate Gift, leaving them martyrs (witnesses) of the good news for others. This is central to the spirituality of ordinary people.

Ordinary people need a spirituality of receptiveness. This in not spiritual greed but the discovery of a purpose to the inner emptiness. Only a receptive spirit can be filled. "Moses withdrew into the wilderness, and there wrapped in quiet silence was united with God" (Gregory of Nyssa).

The discovery of this inner silence enables us to distinguish between created reality and God. Out of the silence flows the creative activity of the Spirit, the "word" we express with our lives. We may say that we are not geniuses, that we do not have the exceptional gift. True enough. The mind is there and the will, but genius is blocked by many things: physical and emotional limitations, lack of training, poor environment, flawed motivation. However, when ordinary people are most fully themselves, there is always some unique form of talent. The Holy Spirit is Fire. Christ came to cast that fire on the earth. Troubles purify and refine; they enkindle us to be on fire ourselves with the importance of things. Anselm of Canterbury, filled with this fire, saw that "God is pregnant with a world that is pregnant with the destinies of things to be born." In this scheme of things we are God's midwives. We have a talent to be perfected which will bring to fulfillment part of the world's destiny. It may be of no more importance than a cup of cold water or a smile that we offer to another. But of that, at least, we are capable. It is the freedom to love that we have when our ego is crucified. Whatever we have is God's gift to us and it heals us when we share it. Eckhart wrote:

> There is nothing in God that destoys what has anything of its own. But he fulfills all things. And so we must not destroy within ourselves a trifling and insignificant good for a greater. We should bring the slight to its utmost perfection.

The crucifixion of self-interest which ordinary people experience is brought about by the presence of Christ. We share his passion. Without this purification, all our acts would be the acts of timid people. We cease to be timid when the transformation of our spirit has diminished within us all boasting, fear of failure, compulsiveness and complaining. It is then that our small talent, through the gift of God's spirit, makes our decisions deliberate and our actions pure.

Our actions reveal our aptitude for God. There is music in the air, fire in the firewood, but they must be called forth. The fire of God's Genius lies unkindled within us until we fan the flame. Its purpose is to set the world on fire. "I have come to light a fire on the earth. How I wish the blaze were ignited!" (Lk 12:49).

It takes the Genius of God to open our ears to the Word and our eyes to its beauty. It is this decision to cleanse our eyes and use the power we have of the Spirit which begins the process of our healing.

"Long hunger wasted the world-wanderer, with sight of You may he be satisfied" (Rhadbod).

What To Do

Purpose: To discover the Holy Spirit working within you.

Input: Everybody has a gift—composers, artists—but also ordinary people living down the block.

Sharing: Mention things you save because they have memories. Share how the power of God has guided you life.

Music: Handel's *Fireworks Suite*, Everest 3353.

Quiet time: Reflect on a skill you have, things you like to do, little things as well as great. Reflect on the power of God you possess to touch the lives of others.

End: Pray aloud Sirach 39:12-21.

Longing

The hunger for God is more devouring than loneliness. The longing for God is a cry of the heart which makes loneliness possible. It makes believers of people and helps them to survive.

The vast majority of the world's believers are Jane and John Does, people with life's burdens who are unknown outside their city or village. They are not theologians. They are unaware that a species, theologian, exists. They are not interested in knowing, and did they know, there is no way in which they could decipher the code in which theology is written. In fact, they do not much think that doctrinal beliefs have any relevance for their lives. Much of what they do know is badly distorted. Bad preaching and slanted views seem to stick in people's minds much longer than any word of freedom or hope. It isn't that they do not have a theology; they do. It lies hidden beneath the instinct they have for life and for survival.

The God they really worship dwells in the struggles of their daily existence, not in the jargon of professional theologians. For the most part their God is silent and acts in silence, nudging them forward through the confusions and complexities of their lives. They have a holy wisdom which supports them in terrible times and gives them courage when wonderful things happen.

When he came to see me, John had just come off a marriage which was a disaster of his own making. He drank too much. He said that now he had met the woman of his dreams, the only woman in the world who could make him happy. The thought of his making her happy did not seem to arise. They were troubled people, both in their 50s. Jane had the kind of eyes which saw a long way into hell; she had dark circles around them to prove it. John was in love, or thought he was, but already Jane was having reservations which she discussed with the pastoral associate, a sister.

John came to discuss the finer points of canon law as they applied to his case. We began by discussing the weather, mortgages, the cost of pickups and other such matters before getting down to business.

"*I was sitting in the Palouse having a drink,*" *he said,* "*when I remembered the dog was in the back of the pickup. It's a '78 Chevy. They don't make them like that anymore.*"

"*I guess.*"

"*So I took the dog down and dropped him off at Lulu's.*"

"*Who's Lulu?*"

"*Lulubell, you know...*"

"*Oh...*"

"*I got back to the Palouse at a quarter of eight; I remember looking at the clock. Jane was there, sitting at the bar with another man.*"

Tears filled his eyes.

"She came right over, I guess she knew how I felt. 'He's only a friend,' she said."

"Yes."

"I turned my back on her and walked right out of there and got in the pickup. I drove down to the river and parked. I had the gun in the pickup. I thought I would just finish myself off to spite her."

"I understand."

"But I wouldn't give her the satisfaction. You don't know, Father, what women are like."

"I have an idea."

"I love that woman so much. If it wasn't for God I'd kill her."

He paused for a moment and wiped his eyes.

"I went back to the Palouse, and the guy was gone. She was there, smoking and drinking coffee. I told her the dog was down at Lulu's. She said that if I liked we could go out with the pickup and get the brass bed and move it in..."

"The brass bed?"

"It's the one she saved from her first mariage."

"Oh."

The conversation continued as I pried out of him the information I needed.

"Well, what we've got here is what's called a formal case. It will take more than a year to process it through the matrimonial court. I guess you'll hardly wait a year?"

"Well, you know, it wouldn't be right in the sight of God to just live together. We'll find someone who can do it."

"Yes, but..." I shut up. I had no right to place him in some kind of false conscience. And there was little hope that the relationship would survive for very long.

A month later, Jane came to the rectory door and asked to speak to Margie.

"It's all over, Margie," she said. "We've separated. These are the satin sheets we got for our honeymoon. I want you to have them," handing over a package.

"The sheets...?" Margie replied with a celibate shudder.

Holding the package gingerly, she invited Jane in, passed her the kleenex and talked to her sympathetically about the seamy side of romance.

After Jane had left, Margie entered my office and asked with a frown, "What am I supposed to do with these?" Her discomfort was entertaining, and she didn't appreciate my smirk.

"You know, for the first time I'm beginning to appreciate something."

"Which is...?"

"Country music. It used to make me sick. Now, I think, maybe it has a theology...something to do with troubled people's solitude?"

God speaks to John and Jane, though they have difficulty reflecting on it, or even recognizing it. They do little in the way of reflective thinking, though they are bright enough. The most uninstructed of people have genuine religious experiences where God touches their lives. Life itself is a religious experience, though people do not realize that and would never say they were religious people. It is not a matter of some born-again experience. There are times when the most secular event or thing becomes transparent with the power and presence of God, with the call to self-transcendence. It is a hierophany, a showing forth of the sacred. Ordinary people have these experiences, though they do not reflect on them. They are hidden in the ordinary moments of their unselfish struggles.

"I am not a very religious person," Jane told Margie one day. "I rarely show up on a Sunday morning."

"Oh, but you are, Jane. You must not confuse being religious with the practices of religion. There are moments when the meaning of your life is there before your eyes. You know what is important and what is phony?"

"Yes, I can feel that at times."

"Those are the times we can see that a selfish world is a sham. We could not see that if we were not in contact with God."

"There are times when I feel real, that God has forgiven me. I feel free."

"Many people feel trapped. Without some contact with God, life has no meaning. We need a way out. People think that money can do it, or a more important job, but these are only things. They trap us as easily as our wild feelings.

"Well, it's like with John. There was a moment there when I felt free. I thought I could get close to him and help him. I guess I should have known that it wouldn't work."

"Maybe it did work...for a while. Having something to offer to another person opened your heart. When you reached out without counting the cost it was a religious moment. Even in your hopeless offer of love to John, wanting to care for him, you became whole with God."

"I know. For a while I was at peace with everybody."

"We have to have something to offer. People who have nothing to offer let themselves die."

"I know. I've been there too. God is close to those who have nothing left. I could have killed myself, but for God. I had no way out from being trapped within myself. It's when I lost everything that I learned to share. It's the way God set me free."

"Yes, hell is having no love to offer. You did OK trying to love John."

"If I could love him, I could love anybody. Is the offer of myself the only way I'll ever love God?"

"Perhaps not the only way, and you do have to be more discerning in the way you go about it. But, yes, it is the way we know God. I'm sure that next time you'll do it more wisely."

Self-giving is our way out. It liberates us into the Infinite. Should the moment be pure, the world will be transparent and what is sacred will be revealed.

God lives in the hearts of Jane and John Doe and speaks to them in silences. Jane stops in to church after work and lights a candle—one has to have ritual, since without it one is left with endless talk. She sits on the hard bench with her littleness and helplessness, her head bent. She tries to put it all together with God. There is inner resistance and tears, then surrender and acceptance. Sometimes in the quiet of the church there is a sense of presence and power; always there is some of that peace the world cannot give. Then, out into the madness again, the noisy street, the shortage of cash, the betrayals and the whole cycle of struggle and event which is grist for God's mill. That mill, the proverb tells us, grinds slowly but it grinds surely. Slowly there comes compassion, understanding, the absence of fear and the presence of hope. In the end there is only life itself to offer, and the elderly surrender it in peace. Their longing is at last fulfilled.

What To Do

Purpose: To get in touch with your hunger for God.

Music: Mahler's *4th Symphony,* Phillips 7300 209.

Quiet time: Close your eyes.
Reflect on your hungers, drives, obsessions.
Are you really ever satisfied?
Is that all?
You were made for God;
only the All of God will satisfy you!

Share: Childhood and teen crushes.
The experience of being in love.
Discuss: "The hunger for God is more devouring than loneliness."

End: Read Psalm 40 aloud, skipping verses 14-15.

Searching

Susan drives downtown in a compact car. She is going somewhere, but she is troubled.

"Where are you heading today, Susan?" I ask.

"Out of my mind," she replies abruptly, but with no intention of being unkind. All is not well with her world. Her friends wonder aloud, "What has gotten into her, she's never satisfied?"

Susan's condition is played out in the lives of thousands of troubled people every day. What is not evident to them is that their condition contains a great deal of good theology awaiting exploration.

Many of Susan's friends are satisfied with life. Their Christianity has made an easy bedfellow with the values of a world closed in on itself. They do not want to be annoyed by the unrest in Susan's life. They do not want to hear of poverty, immigration, poor housing, the nuclear problem, consumerism or other social injustices. Those, they feel, are the concerns of people in high places. They wonder why Susan cannot be like them and enjoy the good life.

Susan is searching for meaning, and the world as she experiences it is not answering her needs. She knows enough by now to suspect that the American dream and living happily ever after have very little to do with following Christ. Her friends want her troubles to cease. Fortunately for Susan, they will not easily cease. There is a spirit of restlessness within her which is a challenge. It has nothing to do with money, position or any form of self-satisfaction. Susan's search cannot be satisfied with anything finite. It is a hunger for absolute fulfillment, for the Infinite. What has "gotten into her" is God's Spirit, though she hardly grasps that and could never spell it out in terms of a spirituality.

At first sight Susan's needs seem modest enough, even somewhat superficial. But we come to the real need when we dig a little deeper.

"My life seems so worthless," she says. "I feel like our old dog who cannot get going in the morning. I want to do something worthwhile, something that would make people sit up and take notice. But I can't get myself going."

"Susan, I haven't yet met a person who did not dream of doing something significant. Most of us never get around to it."

"How come?"

"Well, we think that the significant thing we have to do is outside ourselves. So we excuse ourselves by saying that we do not have the talent or the time. I would see this restlessness of yours as a call to remake your inner self. And you do have the talent to do that. It's a summons from the Creator God to be a co-creator."

"That sure sounds like a tall order."

"Not that tall, Susan. No matter what the circumstances of your life might be, it is something you can do because God supplies the talent. You will continue to be troubled until you do that one worthwhile thing.

This search of yours is an experience of God calling you to inner growth.

"I hope so...I don't know."

"How else would God speak to you in a personal way except through your own experience?"

"I think something is happening within. I know that I would like people to accept me like I was OK, a good person. Then I do something stupid, maybe at a party or somewhere, and I think, 'God, I'm awful.'"

"You're not awful, Susan. You're OK. I'd like to hear you say, 'I'm a good person.'"

"I can't...or I don't want to...it sticks in my throat."

"But it is true. You have to realize that you are a good person just because you want to be good, like people are evil because that is what they want. It isn't so much what you do; it is an inner attitude, a sort of goodness you bring to what you do."

"I try to be good."

"I wish you could see that your sense of being good is your awareness of the Holy Spirit within you. It is God's healing and loving presence."

"There are things I have done.... I'm confused. I mean it when I say I think I'm going out of my mind."

"Don't complicate it. Let what you've done wait for a while. That can be taken care of. Forget about what other people think. It hurts, of course, when they think poorly of us. But we are in good company; Jesus was hurt. Hurt can help us to stop focusing all our attention on ourselves. Your conflicts will end the day you decide to look out there at the hurts of others and decide to do something about them. If Christ has chosen you for himself, you must share in his saving role."

"That's all very idealistic. My problems are more basic than that. I have real problems with God. When I talk to him, he acts like he's dead."

"Maybe that 'he' god never existed."

"There's no response at all. I try looking into his eyes, and I see nothing. I get mad, and he doesn't seem to care. I get on my knees and plead, and there's only silence. How can I deal with somebody like that?"

"Maybe your image of God is childish, something you learned when you were young, an old grandpa in heaven with a white beard? Or God as the Secretary of Health and Welfare. We have to solve our own problems, Susan, even when we do so with God's help."

"Meaning...?"

"Meaning that God is our collaborator. God is on our side, within us. Why don't you try thinking of God as Loving Wisdom. The Loving Wisdom is personal and saturates every cell of your body, every deep place of your spirit. Your problems are Its concerns. Let the Loving Wisdom look out through your eyes at the problems. It will help you solve them."

"But, God does have an objective reality...I mean, apart from whether people believe it or not?"

"Of course, but not as some kind of thing-object in space and time. We cannot lay hold on God the way we lay hold on things. God lays hold on us. This may seem like a crazy example...but it's like getting the flu. You don't get it by studying the virus or reading about it. It gets you. One of these days, after a long struggle with the dark side of your life, you will find that you have been caught by Loving Wisdom. You have already been caught, but you do not realize it yet."

"Perhaps..." Susan doubted aloud. "I search for God, or for evidence to make God responsible for the terrible things that happen. I'm not sure I can find either."

"Susan, you have to sit in the solitude beyond all space. It is there that Loving Wisdom will come to you. What I'm saying is that you have to pray."

"I've done that, too, and it scared me half to death."

"What was it that scared you?"

"The closeness. It only happened once or twice. I backed off so fast, I nearly tripped over myself."

"Scared of your shadow, huh?"

"Maybe God is my shadow, I don't know. If anyone had told me that I'd react so violently to God's presence, I wouldn't believe it. Anyway, who knows in the half-light what the full light might reveal?"

"You mean...about yourself?"

"About myself, and about God also."

"Besides the closeness, what was it that bothered you?"

"Well, I felt that God had come to put all the broken parts of my life back together, and I panicked. It was like there was something inside me that struck out at God...you think I'm possessed or something?"

"No, Susan, that Satan stuff is malarkey, at least the way you think of it."

"I was afraid I'd lose control. I think, maybe, I don't want to solve my troubles."

"Perhaps. We are all victims of a world that wants nothing to do with God. If God put the broken parts of the world together, it would discover that it had to worship. God is its meaning."

"You mean it would lose control?"

"Partially that. Mostly, the world likes being the object of its own obsessions, its stuggle for power. There is something of that in all of us. If it ever accepted the God we know in Christ, it would have to be humble. Its autonomy would be conditional...It would have to be just and make peace. It reacts violently to that. It would be more free, of course, but it would have to worship."

"Do I fear worshipping God?"

"Probably. We all have obsessions we hate to surrender. If you will forgive a bit of frankness, both you and the world fear that if you gave God due honor, God would rape you."

"God wouldn't do that...?"

"I know. But it's what people imply when they accuse God of responsibility for the terrible things which happen. Loving Wisdom would never do that."

"To be honest, I've often accused God of being responsible for some of the evil things in the world."

"It's bad theology. God always respects our freedom."

"I'm not all that free. I have fears...even about the Loving Wisdom you mention...that I'll be seduced some way or other into something I don't want. I might have to give up something."

"Well, it's the word Jeremiah used, 'You have seduced me, Yahweh, and I have let myself be seduced'" (Jer 20:7, *JB*).

"I feel safe so long as there is something there between us, like when I say, 'I know God loves me because others love me.' But if I didn't have something there between us, how could I hold out? You know...to be loved absolutely as you say God loves—mentally, emotionally, spiritually—would destroy me."

"You might lose control, but not your freedom. You keep forgetting that God is Loving Wisdom. Loving Wisdom perfects you from within. It does not absorb you. You do not lose your personality. There is no need to panic, Susan."

"But what if the Wisdom sees that suffering is good for me, that I have to make up for all the things I've done?"

"Suffering is neither good nor bad. What one does with it purifies one or makes one bitter. I don't even know that it's inevitable, though we all seem to get some of it. It does not come from God. Such a God would be a monster. There is no reason to fear God. And as for the things that you have done, God has canceled the debt through the sufferings of Christ."

"But the Bible talks a lot about the fear of the Lord...?"

"Yes, mostly it is a poor translation for 'awe of the Lord,' not the fear which makes us scared and suspicious. And anyway, the people of the Bible improved their idea of God as time went by. Would you fear Jesus?"

"No."

"There is much to be purified in us, but we need not fear that. Somehow, those who give themselves to God seem to find the strength to cope with it."

"So...why am I afraid?"

"Well, because you have to respond to a terrible love, and you are unable to control it. Love and wisdom have no uses, and most of us like to use and control everything."

"They have no uses...?"

"They are not objects to be used for our own advantage. God isn't an object. Loving Wisdom holds you in its embrace, in the fullness of who you are. It gives you life and creativity. It establishes you in your deepest worth. God is meaning, your meaning, not someone to be used and controlled."

"I guess I'm not trusting enough to accept that embrace. And I fear God's solitude, like you said, 'the solitude beyond all space.' I search, but I'm afraid that if I find what I'm searching for, I'll drown in it."

"Susan, it was Loving Wisdom which brought the world to birth. It pushed it out of the solitude into existence. To fear the solitude is to fear the very experience where the scattered parts of your life will be put together again. It is the place of your new creation."

"I think that in spite of the pain I've become comfortable with my troubles. I know who I am with them; I don't know who I should be without them. I guess you won't let me stay there?"

"No, the solitude brings freedom and strength. Everyone has something vital to accomplish in the world, a vital task. Essentially, it is a mission to make something out of ourselves. And we cannot do this except through making something out of somebody else. If we fail this task, our lives will remain unfinished."

"I've been in the solitude you mention. To be honest, what I felt was a sort of ashamed embarrassment, a kind of indignity in being stripped of everything. I had the feeling that God would not do this to us were we not his impoverished people. I don't see him doing it to the rich."

"Oh, I think there are ways in which they experience it also. The problem, Susan, is that we have to be dead before we can be brought back to life again. There is no resurrection without death...I mean, in the spiritual life. We are stripped only of what comes between us and God. You have to accept that kind of solitude in your life."

"Why me?"

"Because people like you have more promise. Let me try to explain: The indignity you speak of is your reduction to formlessness. Life, love and wisdom have no forms. They are formative. They shape your essential being; they make a person out of you. In just the same way, God is formative. So, to be like God, you must be stripped of all form, that is, of your phony self-image. It is only then that you become a maker with God. You regain your dignity when you become like God: formative. For the time being, you will have to go on struggling with the dispossession of your deepest self. Do not avoid it or cover it up with noise or superficial activity. You cannot avoid it. God will conquer your deepest self."

"It scares me."

"Susan, there are two sides to everything, even to absolute love. It is scary when we hear God say to us: 'All that is yours is mine,' but it is ecstasy when we realize the truth of the words, 'All that is mine is yours.' Who can give all without being terrified? And who can receive All without losing control?"

"But...there are those beautiful things that God has given us, are there not? I listen to music and see splashes of color. I smell the flowers and reach for the touch and taste of things. Are they not God's gifts also to win our love?"

"Yes, many people think that God's love is platonic, something purely of the mind. In fact, it is also very sensual and personal. All these things are words spoken by God, but they are only vision. God is more than vision."

"This personal side of God...I don't always like this 'standing at the door and knocking.' There are times when I would like to be left alone."

"That sounds a bit like guilt to me."

"That, too. Like I said, there are things I have done."

"You are loved for yourself, Susan, not for your performance or in spite of it. And you are loved the way you are, not the way you'd like to be. God's love is pure."

"I feel that God's love is a judgment on me."

"There's some truth in that. But Jesus calls us friends. Friends call us to accountability, but not to condemnation. That is God's judgment. The world, as God sees it, is like a handicapped child. It is sad, not something evil to be condemned."

"I understand that sadness. A child has more need to be loved than to be fed. A child who isn't loved injures herself and those about her. It isn't that she's angry, but that she's sad. You're saying that's the way the world is? Maybe the way I am?"

"The world is more sad than angry. It's because it doesn't know the love of God. The poor who know God's solitude are often the more joyful. Go into the poverty of your heart and you will find joy. It is there that God loves you."

"It is there I find pain."

"I think the pain is a side issue, a surface side of healing. God is a surgeon who operates on our wounded condition, but only to heal. God knows your pain. And joy comes with healing."

"I guess so. Sometimes when I listen to music I seem to know how passionately God loves the world."

"We have to have passion, or we'll do nothing well. Music reveals the composer's passion; the world reveals God's passion. You are a person of passion, or you would not feel so deeply. Listen to the music of your own heart. Do not allow the fears to be the determining factor in your life. Accept the solitude for now and it will destroy the power of the obsessive fears. Everyone has dark days."

"I know. But I keep longing and searching for the light."

"It's there already, waiting to be uncovered. It shines every time you love wisely and your wisdom is loving. Listen to your heart, to your search, and you will hear God's passionate music. God already listens to it within you."

"Well, I feel better. I think I can keep struggling."

"Of course you can. But you must not spend your whole life struggling. It would be helpful if you listed all the people, places, happenings and things which give you joy, which energize you, and make up your mind deliberately to cultivate them. Don't take them for granted. Develop what makes you happy."

"I'll do that."

What To Do

Purpose: To discover a more authentic meaning in your life.

Share: What it is that makes life meaningful for most
people—fame, fortune, youth, health, money.
How you have grown over the years.
What wisdom and love you now have that you
did not have as a teenager.

Music: *Rampal plays Bach,* Everest 3383.

Quiet time: Reflect on what it is in you that is most
authentic and honest.
Reflect on what you can develop to be
more positive about the future.

End: Read the Beatitudes aloud: Matthew 5:3-12.

Grief and Letting Go

Juan Domingo Jacinto was a catechist in his village in Guatemala. He was honored by the people, entrusted with the religious education of their children. But he was a marked man, too, as were all who advanced the cause of the poor. His name was on a list. Any night, now, the soldiers might come, break down his door and drag him away never to be heard of again.

Tipped off in time, Juan fled his village leaving behind him a wife and child. The month was November. He walked most of the journey up through Mexico, arriving at the border of the United States in May. By mid-June he was in Idaho, 30 pounds lighter, a small man with bright eyes.

Juan Domingo does not speak English. He has no money and cannot find work. Yet he is cheerful and prayerful. He kneels in church, his head bowed on his hands. One would think that he did not have a care in the world. Perhaps having lost everything there is nothing else to lose?

People pass him on the street. They do not know his name. They do not ask if he has found work, if he has eaten today. Quite simply, they do not even see him. Juan in not envious. He does not covet our superfluous possessions. He would like to work.

When his condition is brought to the attention of the parishioners, the vast majority are sympathetic and offer their help. A few get angry and want him deported back to Guatemala. It's not their fault, they say, that his own people want to kill him. And America belongs to us, not to the likes of him.

As we eat hamburgers at the A & W, I mention in broken Spanish that a friend of mine, Sr. Rachel, is teaching school this summer in Atitlán. Juan looks up quickly from his hamburger, his whole face beaming: "Ah, si," he responds, "Atitlán es muy alegre." ("Atitlán is very happy.") It is his way of saying that Attilán is very beautiful. Having heard his story of loss and grief, I am suddenly ashamed and angry. I wonder why it is that the destitute are treated as if they are of no account, when clearly they are more gentle and loving than the rest of us, and their cities are happy.

Grief is not confined to death alone. There are many reasons why people grieve: the loss of home or a job, the experience of divorce, a humiliation inflicted by another person. Mostly, however, we grieve for the loss of loved ones.

Bereavement, grief, sadness and mourning are spiritual problems. If they are handled with honesty, they precede a new growth in our lives.

Depression is a psychological problem. It may have its roots in a chemical imbalance in our body. It may also originate in our thought processes, in an unwillingness to forgive, in self-pity, low self-esteem, faulty or rigid thinking. It may come from resentment which accompanies an unpleasant home or work environment. It needs professional help.

There is a need to mourn. Grief of one kind or another is a large part of our ordinary condition. When we suffer a major loss we go through a process of change. This is a spiritual journey. We do have to remember that mourning is a process, not a state of being. A process has a history, it is going somewhere, it is a journey. But when mourning becomes its own purpose, we have a state of being. If we view our sorrow as an end in itself, a way of life, there is no reason why it should ever end. We can always find reasons for prolonging it. Misery becomes a lifestyle. We torture ourselves and make others miserable. They have every right, for our good and theirs, to tell us to end it and get on with our lives. There is infinitely more to life than the greatest and most painful loss.

There are those who deny the loss in a variety of ways. Denial lies be-hind anger, denunciation of others and blaming God. Anger with God is largely self-indulgent and very bad theology. From the point of view of spirituality, it is immature. Loss has to be confronted. Confronting the reality with maturity enables us to see that this loss is not the totality of our experience. When the loss is of a person or persons, their absence allows us to love them for themselves and not for what they were for us. The previous togetherness went as far as it would go. We should leave it there. Daydreams about where it might have gone are unreal. We let go of that luxury. There is no growth until we let go.

We have our memories, of course, but memory is a tricky thing. It is a blessing to have happy memories. Yet memories are always a selection we make from the past. They are not the reality. The reality was some-thing and someone vastly greater. The danger lies in constructing a memory and unconsciously accepting it as the whole of what the past has been. The problem is not in having memories but in making them the whole of our reality. If we grieve for a divorced or deceased person, we should remember that the person has gone into our future. No one who has been loved is entirely lost. The future reign of God, our only fu-ture, will restore the love. The person we mourn no longer lives in the past of dead memories, but resides in our future. The dead have not abandoned us. They are coming toward us as we go forward to meet them.

Memories are images. We need to shape our life's meaning. But the memory of a loved one should never become greater than the real per-son. For example: in church the image of a holy person sometimes be-comes a "holy image." People couldn't care less for the saint, but don't you dare touch that statue. It is the holy image. Something like this happens with the image of the loved person we lost. Nobody is allowed to touch the memory. It is cherished and hugged more closely than the person ever was in real life. The fact is that the past was never that perfect. There were bad moments and events. They also are part of the reality. We should grieve for the loss of the person and not for the presence of memories. The person is sacred, the memories only a construct.

Grief should not be passionate for long. Passionate grief destroys reality and makes love impossible. It is too self-conscious; it does nothing to unite us with the person we loved. St. Paul urged against grieving as those who have no hope (1 Thes 4:13). Our hope is in Christ who remembers all the lost members of his body.

When we refuse to let go, we inevitably dramatize and ritualize our refusal in some symbolic fashion. It might be in letting things slide. We say that nothing matters anymore. We may become unconcerned with our appearance, our work may become careless, we eat and sleep less, we make others pay by rudeness and anger. Thoughts of suicide enter our mind. Such grief is too self-focused. It is, perhaps, inevitable; it is also a time for our friends to keep us honest. Our destruction is not an act of love for the person we loved. It adds nothing to such a person. There is a disappointing factor in C.S. Lewis's A *Grief Observed*. He tells us that he shall be a one-legged man for the rest of his life. That is a weakness. It is not a necessary fact; it is a decision and a choice. It is true that we can never be the same again. But who wants to remain the same all through life? We can grow and be better people as a result of a loss. The choice is ours. A new unforeseen and creative life lies before us. But only if we let go.

Christ told his disciples to let go, that if they did not the Spirit would not come to them. It is not too much to anticipate a way in which the spirit of a separated person returns to us, provided we let go. A new and more unselfish love is made possible. Lewis rightly saw that feelings of presence and unusual experiences of the departed are quiet suspect. Yet he ends his account by accepting just such an experience. But that is not the gift of the spirit. The more valid experience is the discovery of our new self, who and what we become as we go bravely into the future.

We ask basic questions: "Where is she now?" Such a question does not make much sense—the only reply would have to do with personal freedom—but it has to be asked. Or we ask, "What shall I be without him?" or "What shall I do?" The answers come slowly. They are faith questions because they have to do with ultimate reality. Only faith can make sense of loss. The discoveries which result from our questioning are made as our faith grows, and we ourselves change. The person we lost through death or abandonment is in a new condition of being. We let go of the past and accept that condition. We may cry in our hearts, "Come back!" but would return be better for the departed? We let go of presence so that growth might be possible.

We must also let go of the pain. Neither God nor the loved person is the source of our pain. Pain is personal. It may be good. It refines us, purifying all that is self-interested. When it has done its work, we should rid ourselves of it. Life was given to us to be celebrated. Hugging the pain of separation to ourselves for too long becomes masochistic. There are those who feel that letting go of the pain is a betrayal of the person they loved. They feel guilty. But grief is not helping the departed person, and it does not bring them back. There is nothing to be guilty about. And wondering with anxiety whether the person is in God's good graces is something of a presumption. God is more powerful to save than people's misbehavior is to damn. We should not play the judge on others. A good sleep and some decent food will do more to help us remember with joy the blessing that was ours in the people we loved. It will also help restore the upset balance of our private world.

We should seek whatever facilitates the arrival of our new person, the richer personality which develops with the grieving process. Giving grief time allows us to discover our limitations and furthers the discovery of new ways to cope. It is then that we can celebrate. It is our summons to holiness. Letting go of loved people, places or events is painful, but it purifies and expands our spirit. It makes us beautiful.

What To Do

Purpose: To transcend loss.

Input: The person you lost has gone into your future
and is now coming toward you.
What you remember of the past is only a selection,
not the entire reality. Do not live in it.

Sharing: Mention the good things of the past, but also
the things you are tempted to exclude from memory.
Are you doing something to deny the loss?
What is it that makes letting go of it so difficult?

Music: Beethoven's *Violin Concerto in D Major, Op. 61.*
Larghetto movement. Allegro tape ACS 8044.

Reflection: Nothing that was ever loved is ever ultimately lost.
It will return.
What gift of the Spirit is now being offered to you
so that you will become a new and greater person?

End: Read aloud John 16:20-33.

Celebrating Trouble

When Harriet died, the funeral director called and made arrangements for the vigil service and the Mass of Christian burial. Harriet had led a troubled life, and the trouble carried over into death.

The chief mourner at the vigil service was a dog, a small, white one with a mean disposition. A friend of Harriet's held the dog on his lap in the first seat of the front row of mourners. Before the service began, the family called me aside to explain about the dog. It was Harriet's closest friend. It had no competition from the family—the way she saw it. She had made it clear that "they had done ceased" to have the qualities of loyalty, affection and understanding possessed by her pet. The mourners were aware of that and discussed it openly in my presence. Now that she was dead, they wished to honor her requests.

Harriet left instructions in her will that on the occasion of her death the dog was to be "put to sleep," placed in her arms in the casket and buried with her. This seemed reasonable to all but a few of the mourners. The funeral director was less sure, but was prepared to do the necessary thing to avoid hurting anyone's feelings.

The family informed me that they had discussed the pros and cons of the matter and wished to honor the request. On the pro side it was argued that the dog was only a dog, that it had no claim to continued existence in view of Harriet's explicit request. On the con side it was argued that the dog had not ever lived a dog's life, that it had undergone a certain apotheosis and was now endowed with the human qualities of loyalty, friendship and fidelity. As I listened I marveled at the rapid development of myth. After anguished discussion a compromise was reached which satisfied everybody. It was agreed that a picture should be taken of the dog. This was placed in the hands of the deceased so that, as they explained, when she got to the other side it would be the first thing she saw.

After the matter was explained to me, I walked up to the casket and peered in. The snapshot was in her hands, propped up to face her closed eyes. She was wearing glasses.

Periodically during the service, the dog's upper lip would curl back in a growl, baring sharp teeth. There was no reaction from the solemn-faced mourners. They seemed to understand the dog.

We celebrate life, death and separations because we are troubled and oftentimes desperate people. The only other option we have is to despair.

There are many ways of celebrating, many of them self-indulgent. The self-indulgent celebrations are not our concern here. There is no growth in them, just a dulling of the pain and an escape into blissful unconsciousness.

It would be reassuring to think that our better celebrations are of resurrection. But resurrection in our daily living is such a self-transcendent thing that one doubts whether it is celebrated consciously very often, or at all. We see something of it in the return of the hostage, the glorification of the hero, the office party following the return of someone after an illness. These events call forth a moment of unselfish gratitude, and people celebrate.

Where God comes into it on the level of radical solitude is where people are desperate. Life is desperate for thousands of troubled people. And in the teeth of that desperation there is a fierce need to celebrate. Not to celebrate would be a capitulation to despair. So, someone wants to kill a dog or a bull. One hears the despair in bullfight music; one sees it in the bravado. "Olé, let us be merry, tomorrow we die."

It is true. We shall all die tomorrow. There shall be no survivors. To have loved this earth and its people passionately, and to have to leave it, is a despairing situation. We might fall into the philosophy or theater of the absurd with Sartre and Samuel Beckett and capitulate: "Life has no meaning, we all must die." But that solves nothing. We need a faith that only God can supply. So, out we go and kill a bull, or kill Jesus Christ, because we are desperate. It is ourselves we are killing, of course. We know that. We cannot endure the loss. It is better to kill a bull than kill ourselves. We kill the bad guys every night on TV. They are our surrogates. Somehow we shall survive.

I recall my first experience of a person's death. A woman near home died. I was 7 years of age and brought to the wake because it was proper that we should honor the deceased. Pipes of tobacco and glasses of whiskey were passed around to the men, glasses of sherry to the women. This was done not for the sake of drinking alcohol but for the sake of celebrating the desperate situation: "Drink up, now, an' 'twill take the chill off your bones. Sure, 'tis the end we're all coming to." I sat in the bedroom where the body was laid out. I stared at the gray face of the dead woman. I had known her, but did not know death. Then, a housefly alighted on her upper lip and crawled up into her nostril. I was fascinated by the sight and I waited for the sneeze. She didn't sneeze. I knew that had she been alive she would have sneezed. Death was a lifeless corpse. She was not there. The wake went on through the night, long after the family members were urged to get some sleep. An endless flow of stories and humor was shared. It was all whistling in the dark. We cope with mystery and desperation by celebrating.

We still do it with circus clowns. We are all clowns in face of the troubles of living and dying. We need the clowns; they are ourselves. People of faith are all "fools for Christ's sake" (1 Cor 3:18). A woman whose marriage has failed goes out and has an affair, not because she is immoral but because she is desperate. It isn't that she needs the man. She knows that. What she does not know is that in this bizarre behavior she is desperately seeking God. Will she find God? Perhaps not. Will God find her? Well, Jesus found many like her in Judea and Galilee, and he understood. What he rejected was the hypocrisy of the person whose want of love drove other people into such behavior.

If you are the sort of hapless person who goes to a football game and sits there uninvolved while all around you people are stomping and screaming and slurping beer, you are, possibly, called to another option. The symbolical struggle between good and evil on the field is very much part of all of us. It is quite understandable that the mildest of men cry: "Break his bones; jab him in the ribs." The same words were used for Jesus on the cross. Christ accepted it without bitterness or revenge. That is the only other option, assuming that the theater of the absurd is dead. Nor is this a capitulation. It is the dignified acceptance of the harshness of reality until such time as we can change it for the better.

This was Jeremiah's insight when he went to the potter's shed and watched the potter break and remake his vessels. When God sees that the work of our making fails, God allows us to be broken. The story does not end there. We are broken to be remade. Our moments of desperation need not be covered up with loud cries of bravado. We can accept our breaking, and anticipate the arrival of our new person. If we have turned out less than our potential would anticipate, God owes it to us to remake us. Not that God steps in and does it personally—life does it. But then, all of life works within God's providence, drawing good from evil.

We do not want to change. Despite our troubles, we want to return to the way things were before we were hurt. This is understandable since the past is the only experience we know. We do not even know if there shall be a new person. But death must precede resurrection, which is the arrival of the new personality. No one can successfully return to the past. What may happen is that we get bogged down in an endless struggle, never making a decision. Our resistance to growth and change can only be overcome by a decision.

Decision-making is our celebration of trust in God in troubled times. It is more than a change of opinion or of moral judgment. It involves our whole person in our relationship with God. We begin with an unconditional acceptance of ourselves just as we are, without excuses or qualifications. We accept the reality of our weakness, limited understanding and obsessive fears. In this situation we are forced to rely on a power greater than ourselves so as not to be crippled by the troubles of the human condition. Now we are ready to move on into being a new and more realistic person. When God breaks the vessel—figuratively speaking—we hear a summons to expand the narrow limits of our lives. These narrow limits are usually imposed on us by other people. Now we must move out of the sheltered existence to something new. We alone may say what that decision will be.

To be of any value, this celebration of the transcendence of limits must be a journey out of ourselves into God—not merely rebellion and revolt. It is a quiet and unshakeable celebration of the triumph of human dignity and trust over despair. It is a celebration because it is a surprised awakening to possibilities we have always known but were reluctant to act upon. We are not called by God to be the doormats of any oppression or addiction.

The actual moment of decision takes place when we hit bottom, when we say, "No more." It is the moment of helplessness, purification and freedom. It is the moment when Christ dies on our cross. It has to be celebrated by our choice to die into resurrection, to break through into freedom. It is a personal moment of decision taken in the solitude of our heart. It is the small life hidden in the seed which falls to the ground and dies into new life. It is our great moment of history, our incorporation into the saving death of Christ, the beginning of the reign of

God in us, our act of surrender and acceptance of holiness. The mystery of God is interwoven with the life we live and the struggles we endure.

In the face of our torments and doubts, well-meaning people try to support us. They say to our questioning: "But of course your life has meaning. Look at all the good you are doing." This sort of thing will never solve our troubles. A need for affirmation is never-ending. The only ultimate support is in the fact that resurrection alone will vindicate us. And resurrection is God's doing, not ours. In the end, questions about the meaningfulness of life are pointless; they are born of anxiety. We celebrate a less than flattering existence, abandon ourselves to God and get on with the business of living. Life is not glorious. No amount of questioning and no amount of whistling in the dark are going to cover up people's willingness to sacrifice people for their ideals. The less fortunate will be exploited, cheap labor will be defended and building ever more terrible weapons of war will continue. What is there to celebrate? Only that Christ is the way and the truth and the life, and that we have abandoned ourselves to him as our way also. That is a celebration of trouble in hope and freedom.

A robin flew against my window and fell on the veranda fluttering its wings. It struggled to its feet, its beak open, and stood there swaying back and forth trying to get its balance. Then its head dropped slowly and two drops of blood fell from its beak. Something inside me cringed. The robin remained there for more than an hour, its body shaking from its rapid heartbeats. I wondered, "Why all the pain, Lord?"

As far as we are concerned, God has no answer for us. More scandalous still, there is nothing God can do about it. The Creator God who calls us to maturity in an unfinished world refuses the self-serving roles we insist on assigning to the divine. God will not play favorites and abuse the world's freedom. Rapes, physical and mental abuse, accidents and death happen to the most innocent of people every day.

Once more, we are thrown back on Christ. If Jesus is the Word which spoke the terrible solitude of God, then God has shared our pain. The pain has become a divine experience. It has entered God and is for that reason forever saved. Here is where we might find and answer to the suffering of the universe.

After an hour, the robin raised its head. When I returned from lunch it had gone. But its blood is still on the veranda. The blood of Christ is on the hands and feet and sides of troubled people. Do we dare celebrate it?

What To Do

Purpose: To rise above depression or despair.

Share: The things which make you angry.
What people mean by "whistling in the dark."
How people swing from hysterical laughter to
sobbing in times of bereavement.
The times you have gone from anger to acceptance.

Music: Mozart, *Divertimenti*, AMP X 56015.

Quiet Time: Reflect on the sorts of decisions you must
make to prevent your being defeated by life.

End: Read aloud Matthew 6:25-34.

The Call to Holiness

Imagine yourself transported by night to some out-of-the-way place. You are left alone there in darkness. You hear sounds and movement about you. You are terrified. In fact, you might well die of terror, as people do when they can no longer make sense of their world. Unable to control the moment, we have terror of the unknown. This is the troubled state.

Imagine, then, with dawn arising, that you find yourself in a meadow blanketed with wild flowers. Deer and other wildlife are coming awake with the light. You would laugh, perhaps cry, feel foolish and embarrassed and greatly relieved.

This is the way it is with the holiness of God. Without the light we are terrified of its wrath—holiness will not compromise with evil. But with the light we come to see God's mercy—holiness is loving transformation. Our terror of the unknown ceases when we cease to project our fears and angers onto other people.

The holy is God. It fills us with awe and reverence, yet it is a blessing. It repels and hurts us because of our selfishness, yet it attracts us as our only fulfillment. It gives life. When we grasp at it, or try to control it, it rejects us as hypocritical. Yet it is given to the humble of heart who accept it. It is never ours as being "of" us it is beyond measure, "other," and we live because of its mercy. Yet it is our true destiny and our deepest joy. It pains us as it liberates us from our obsessions and addictions, yet it delivers us from emptiness and despair. The Holy is One. We are strangers to it and at home with it.

Holiness cannot be defined. It is not an object. There is no battery of tests to determine those who are and those who are not holy."By their fruits shall you know them," yes, but also "wolves are found in sheeps' clothing." A share in God's life? Yes. But what is God's life? Solitude, self-disclosure and gifted love? On a grand scale, yes.

When we ask, 'What is the meaning of things,' we come across understandings of them as good, true or beautiful. They are the transcendentals which are not diminished by use. Their use, if anything, appreciates them. Is the holy one of them? It also transcends all being, and all things are saturated with it. There is a difference: Things are of themselves good, true and beautiful; they are not of themselves holy. Holiness is always a gift.

A holy thing has more than its goodness or beauty. It stands as a symbol, as something gifted by ultimate purpose. It becomes holy when it is endowed with the power to point back to our original source and forward to our ultimate end. Holiness always embraces the whole meaning of our existence. Holy people, places, things and events answer, each in its own degree, the questions: 'Why are we here? What is it all about?' They are in some measure a disclosure of the Holy One. It might be a saint or a mountain, a "burning bush," a sacred fountain or river, a crucifix, a shrine where someone laid down his or her life for another. It is a disclosure where ultimate meaning is revealed.

The good, the true and the beautiful are values. Of themselves they do not disclose ultimate meaning. Our value system gets a great deal of attention these days. Supposedly if we have the right values we are a credit to society. Basically the idea goes back to Plato for whom values were absolute essences in heaven. They were to be reproduced as far as possible, though feebly at best, here on earth. Were we to reproduce them, we would be like the gods and worthy of admiration. The ego would be intact. There was danger, of course. Too great an ambition in this regard might arouse the envy of the gods and bring swift punishment.

The biblical approach is quite different. It does not tell us to do good because it is a value, still less because it is expedient. The Greek concept of a tension between good and evil is not the concern of the Bible. The Bible's concern is the struggle between holiness and evil. For the Jews these are personal, not mere values. Ordinary people do battle with the evil Principalities and Powers. Their weapon is holiness, the gift of God's Holy Spirit.

"I remember the exact spot on the road," a friend recalled. "I was driving north. I had this powerful sense of God's presence. I realized what I had known all along, that my addiction was destroying myself and my family. I was overwhelmed. I knew that I had responsibilities to God as well as to them. I came to a decision. That was 10 years ago, and I haven't looked back. I never pass that bend in the road without remembering." That is good, but it is more: It is presence and power. So although the good may be a value, it is done not because of its goodness but because we owe it to God. That is holiness. It has to do with the whole sweep of our life, our origin and end. In the average eulogies we endure at funerals, the deceased is praised for being a value to society, a person of high moral standards, a credit to the country. Seldom is one praised for being a fool for Christ's sake. The fool is holy.

The presence of the holiness of God is experienced when normal people discover that they are never alone in the world or in their battle with evil. The Holy One is present in power. It is the Spirit of God transforming the little and weak ones of the world into the reign of God. It points them back to their Source and forward to their fulfillment. It is the moment which transforms our lives. Evil is never overcome by not doing something. Mark Twain is reputed to have said: "It is easy to give up smoking. I've done it a thousand times." Evil is overcome only by doing good as a response to another person, the Holy God. Holiness is uncovered when we realize that we do not belong to ourselves, but to God. Even our bodies are not our own: "You have been bought and paid for. That is why you should use your body for the glory of God" (1 Cor 6:20, *JB*). Before being told in Scripture what is good or evil, we are first called upon to be a holy people, people covenanted to God in love.

The meaning of our existence is holiness. When our lives in all their aspects of work, prayer, love, lifestyle and recreation point clearly to our origin and end, the holy covenant is fulfilled. We break out of the enclosure of self-interest in acts of kindness to others. That freedom is openness to the presence and power of God.

We are all familiar with people who do good for the sake of good. It is not holy, and their charity repels us because there is not a gift of the heart. They never risk breaking out of their pious self-interest. And we know people who are lost in the beautiful, but going to the symphony does not necessarily open one's heart to the poor. It is when, in a moment of goodness and beauty, people also open their hearts in compassion that the holy is revealed. It is then that bodily, spiritually and emotionally we are drawn into the mysterious world reserved for God. We are liberated from slavery to the finite.

This process is called *theosis,* divinization, being made whole and holy. St. Athanasius put it boldly: "The divine Word was made flesh that we might become gods." It is a process of gradual transformation. As God from all eternity brings forth the Son in the Spirit, so in time God brings forth the Son in us through the Spirit. We are growing toward "the full maturity of Christ" (Eph 4:15). "We are called to be by grace all that Christ is by nature" (Maximus the Confessor). "We are creatures who have received a command to be gods" (St. Basil of Caesarea). What they are all saying is that our justification and sanctification are no mere extrinsic titles by virtue of the blood of Christ, but a radical transformation and divinization of our whole person. This does not mean that we are absorbed by the divinity, that we become God. It is not a substantial union but the immediate substantial presence of God in the justified person. As Paul put it, we are one spirit with God (1 Cor 6:17). We are united with God without any created intermediary while remaining our own individual selves. We are united in and to God in a personal relationship, not through anything impersonal. God gives us God, and that gift is sanctifying. Through God's Genius we are able to interiorize Christ before ever we are able to imitate him. St. Augustine wrote in the *Confessions:*

> Late have I loved you, O Beauty ever ancient, ever new! Too late have I loved you. And, behold, you were within, and I abroad, and there I searched for you. You called, and shouted, and burst my deafness.... You touched me and I burn for your peace.

When the holy enters the life of an ordinary person, it is always accompanied with a sense of unworthiness. People feel guilty. How could we feel guilty were we not reflected in the person of the Holy God? This experience is not, necessarily, a sudden inrush of grace, a once-and-for-all deliverance. Peter experienced the presence of the Holy God at the miraculous haul of fish. He knelt and said: "Leave me, Lord. I am a sinful man" (Lk 5:8). It was not to be the end of his sinning. Holiness is the work of a lifetime. We have to trust God who is present in our troubles and unworthiness. It is our growth into being holy people. After all, we are not the authors of holiness: God is.

The gulf between our sinfulness and God's holiness which we are called to share can be crossed by God alone. This asserts that God is "other"; it does not say that being other means that we are separated. The bridge between the Holy God and what is profane in us is a bond which helps us to recognize the holy for what it is: a transformation of our whole being by the presence, power and holiness of God. It is not our doing; it is given whenever we acknowledge our unworthiness.

The holy has nothing to do with self-affirmation, self-interest, ego-building or organizational ability. Rather, it uncovers for us the essential worth of others. It is not an emotion but a sober reality which enables us to love the least of God's little ones. It is inseparable from loving service to others. It is inseparable from the task of perfecting ourselves so as to be worthy of God's poor and wounded people. It will always confirm others in their inner dignity.

Since good deeds done to others are done to God, the holy enables us to interact with God. It is inseparable from some suffering, since it demands self-transcendence. It is received when our sinful center is conquered by God, therefore it is humble. It is not incompatible with personality flaws—a psychotic, neurotic or schizophrenic person may very well be holy. Whether one knows Christ or not, it is inseparable from identification with him.

For some people, holiness reveals its presence in a deep sense of awe before the mystery of God; for others, it is a courageous acceptance of Christ's way of self-emptying (Phil 2:2-8) as their way also. Holiness is the transformation of all that is little and weak into the reign of God. With it comes endurance, forgiveness and a willingness to accept the weaknesses of others. Julian of Norwich wrote this of the holiness of Christ:

> Truly, it is the most joy that be, as to my sight, that he that is highest and mightiest, noblest and worthiest, is lowest and meekest, homliest and most courteous; and truly and verily this marvelous joy shall be shown us all when we see him (*Shewings of Divine Love*).

What To Do

Purpose: To enable you to share God's life and being.

Input: The Holy is God. It is experienced as power and presence. It is Mystery. It transforms the lives of ordinary people.

Sharing: Name some people you think are holy.
What is it about them?
Where is the power and presence of God
experienced in our modern world?

Music: Liszt, *Piano Concerto, No. 1.*

Quiet Time: Focus attention deep within your spirit.
Invite God's power and presence.
Make a choice for the final meaning of your life.

End: Read aloud, 1 John 1:1-7.

God And Demons In The Desert

The desert and the mountain have been religious symbols in the spirituality of people everywhere. They have spoken to people of faith from a time before history was recorded. We go to them to discover what it is that God is saying to us. Every religion has its desert and holy mountain.

We long for the mountains. Our flatland living needs balancing out. The mountain is the exhilarating high place, the "way out" from our everyday drudgery. It is the place where earth meets heaven. The journey to the mountain seems simple enough. We know where our mountain is: It is the height we wish to conquer, the goal in life we wish to achieve. The very thought of future success gives joy. All we have to do is go there, climb it and be set free. On that high level we shall live happily ever after.

But there is a snag. Before we get to our mountain we have to cross the desert. There are, in fact, many deserts, each with its demons.

The desert is the place of our growth and creativity; what we do well comes out of our solitude. But there is another aspect to the wilderness: It is the place of our testing. The desert is our troubled state. It is the dwelling place of our demons. It is only when the demons are held at bay that we have anything original and authentic to offer others. That is why "Jesus was led into the desert by the Spirit to be tempted by the devil" (Mt 4:1). The Desert Fathers—Egyptian and Syrian—went there to do combat (*agon*) with the demons. Their agony and the demons are our own. They are personal, social and religious. Or, at least, they are irreligious in a religious setting.

Before we discover our way out from our human condition, we must risk the wilderness. Our Promised Land, American Dream, Fountain of Youth or Isle of the Blest are not simply dropped in our lap by virtue of our longing alone. The desert journey is a crossing of great labor. The desert is a metaphor of life, the whole of life's journey. So also is the mountain climb.

On the spiritual journey, those who long for God had better be prepared for obstacles. Life is not glorious for troubled people who are divided within themselves. When one desert seems to be crossed, there comes another, whether retirement, old age, illness or death. Jesus was tested, so shall we be, the "servant not being greater than the master." But we can survive. Better still, we can turn the desert into the place of new beginnings. There are days when the sky is cloudless, life is music and our journey a pleasant one. Our heart is singing. It is curious that wherever we are in life, present joy wipes out the cost of getting there. We anticipate good times rather than bad and never cease to be surprised when the testing begins again.

Solitude

The desert has many forms. There are sagebrush deserts, alkali deserts and deserts of blowing sand. There are red-rock deserts and deserts of black volcanic cinders and lava. The Craters of the Moon desert is formed of lava rock which flowed out over the countryside from the many craters. Evidence of enormous fires is everywhere. Whole rivers of molten rock, now cooled and hardened, stream across the land like plaits of hair. The rock is porous; it had been frothing with fiery gas. The craters splattered and exploded into mounds of black cinders, spatter cones and volcanic ash. This solitude is a dark, forbidding place. It wanders off a hundred miles with its fiery heart still beating at a shallow depth beneath the surface. Except for the limberpines, the brittlebrush and the yellow lichens on the rocks, it is a desolate place.

We do not come to the desert "cold." We have attitudes born of stories we have heard or of experiences which we have had. So we learn from the desert what we have been conditioned to learn. The military have found uses for the deserts of Idaho, Utah and California as training places for death and survival. The wealthy have homes in the deserts of Arizona. Others look on the desert as a place to be shunned, as hostile. Still others see it as a place where nature can be studied and appreciated in a unique way. Then there are those who have looked on the desert with reverence: the Christian spiritual masters, the Hopi and the Navaho. It is a place of spiritual resources. The desert is the solitude of God. For all of us, it is not just being in the desert but the manner in which we are there that matters. Our attitude determines what it is the desert has to teach us.

When we arrive at the desert, be that desert physical, emotional or spiritual, we arrive at a threshold. It is a boundary line, the borders of our familiar country, our everyday lived experience. Our first reflection is to wonder what may lie beyond that boundary. Is it alien and hostile or welcoming and informative? The familiar is left behind us as we cross over into the wilderness. We look, listen, concentrate and explore. But this concentration brings about a change in us. The outer journey of our life turns inward. The question now is, Who am I, here in this solitude? We have some knowledge of who we are, and what we are capable of doing, in our everyday experience of life. But here in the desert, our troubled state, we are deprived of all customary feedback. We must dig deeper. Our former "self" is left behind. We seek what is new. We have gone beyond the fixed limits of daily living. We must now identify with, and accept, the new environment. Should we fail to do so, our desert demons will devour us.

We make the inward journey through attentiveness, reflection and questions. The desert is a mirror in which we see a new self reflected. We need the place of solitude to reflect, and we must be true to that solitude. Thoreau wrote: "What business have I in the woods, if I am thinking of something out of the woods?" To go bodily into the desert has as its purpose to be there spiritually, to be present to one's true self. Otherwise we shall be like the man in the Bible who looked in the mirror and then went away and forgot what manner of man he was. The true self is a harmony of togetherness, the inner Christ. This is the self we are seeking in the desert.

The desert was important in the ideas and religious symbolism of Israel. It was there that Israel first met God. Ever since then, exodus, wandering, exile, going out across the borders of the familiar are images of people's encounter with God. The symbol has to do with loss, crisis, testing and coming to our senses in a new world. It is the discovery that we could not have survived had God not been guiding us:

> *"Be careful not to forget the Lord, your God,...who guided you through the vast and terrible desert with its saraph serpents and scorpions, its parched and waterless ground; ...that he might afflict you and test you, but also make you prosperous in the end"* (Dt 8:11-16).

When God's faithful one stumbled and fell, she would be brought back to the desert where God could speak directly to her and recover her love:

> *I will make her like the desert.*
> *reduce her to an arid land,*
> *and slay her with thirst....*
> *I will hedge her way with thorns...*
> *so that she cannot find her path.*

> *I will allure her;*
> *I will lead her into the desert*
> *and speak to her heart* (Hos 2:5,8,16).

Yet it is this very desert of the spirit which will bloom when God comes with saving power:

> *The desert and the parched land will exult;...*
> *They will see the glory of the Lord,...*
> *Say to those whose hearts are frightened:*
> *Be strong, fear not!* (Is 35:1,2,4).

It is in the desert that we find favor with God. It is there that God gave his mission to Elijah. There John the Baptist began his preaching. There Jesus was put to the test and clarified his mission. Paul prepared himself for his life's work in the desert of Arabia (Gal 1:17). It is in the desert that "the woman" (the church) finds a place prepared by God to protect her from a hostile world (Rev 12:6,14). We rediscover God in the testing of our troubled state. We also discover our true self within the self of God in that wilderness.

It would be easy enough to enjoy the rugged beauty of the Craters of the Moon desert without thought of hazard. Hazards there are, scorpions and snakes, if we wander too far among the rocks. Some miles south, a young boyscout wandered off from his troup and got lost. He would be safe enough, his friends said, he had learned survival skills. When they found the body, it had the fang marks of 13 rattlesnake strikes.

This is symbolic of our getting lost in our problems, longing for the former way of life. Our wasteland has its demons of depression, self-pity and anger. The solitude will devour us unless we find a way to be creative in it. We look back at the pain, the silences, the contempt, the insolent looks and remarks, the emotional, perhaps even physical, abuse and say as we remake our world: "No, God does not expect that of anybody. There was nothing Christian in it, in sign or in fact." There were, and there shall continue to be hazards: the tempter, the silence, the scars and the doubting Thomas who says that we did not try hard enough. We have doubts: What am I doing here in the desert? But, then, Jesus descended into the "lower regions of the earth." It was the prelude to resurrection. After the resurrection, the scars were glorious. There was a new creation. Forgiveness, understanding, gentleness and a more compassionate heart are created within us. The Word of the Lord comes out of our solitude, remaking our world.

The Desert of Fear

Beyond the Craters of the Moon lies INEL (Idaho National Engineering Laboratory), commonly referred to as the site. It lies in a vast sagebrush desert which has a lake beneath its surface. The lake is fed by Lost River, so named from its disappearance into the ground. The underground lake supplies the needs of several nuclear reactors. INEL is a weapons laboratory, with the Department of Defense as its biggest source of funding. Military and government nuclear fuels are reprocessed for weapons. A large portion of the transuranic waste handled at the various facilities on the site comes from weapons production factories. The site is some sixty miles across with mountains to the north of it.

Fear is the dominant emotion here. Two SWAT teams, closed-circuit TV, radar and posted signs on the entrances to the private roads give evidence of paranoia. But fear communicates itself. Those who drive across this desert experience anger. It is a reaction to fear. These many nuclear weapons deserts are the places where humans plan the possibility of the final holocaust. This is the desert where the Word is tempted. It is the place where all the world's "words" are scheduled for crucifixion.

Christ remained in the desert for 40 days, "put to the test there by Satan" (Mk 1:13). The three temptations of the Word closely accord with the three great temptations of life: that salvation comes from solving the economic problem, changing stones into bread; from solving the political problem, having all the nations of the earth under one's sphere of influence; from solving the technological problem, having power over the forces of nature. These are the three temptations which Jesus rejected. Despite the three great longings of the human family—those of the hungry, the politically oppressed and the unlettered—and despite his own longing for what would have been an earthly utopia, he opted to commit himself without reservation to the fulfillment of his Father's will. Not that these things are not necessary and important, but that they are not enough. Christ would depend entirely on a higher spiritual power, and view the world in that light. He multiplied bread, instructed the unlettered, walked on water, but his advice was to seek first the reign of God and God's justice (Lk 12:31). As for weapons of war: "All who draw the sword will die by the sword," he observed tersely.

The parallels are obvious: The production and sale of weapons is good for the economy; it turns uranium-filled rock into bread. Our sphere of influence is made possible by our having those weapons. Our power over nature is established by our technology. It was all promised by Satan in return for a false worship which makes them ends in themselves. The nuclear fears and the spiritual desert which demands them are all too real. The missles are our demons. We cannot live without them. We invented death and called it "Peacekeeper."

The Christian communites which tolerate the production of nuclear weapons have failed the temptation. They are getting fat on the desert carrion. Their bellies are full of the bread of worshipping the false god: Missile. "All these," the tempter said, "will I bestow on you if you prostrate yourself in homage before me" (Mt 4:9). We have done so, and he has kept his promise. We are the most powerful nation on earth. There is a price, as there always is with the demonic. It is the death by radiation which follows the death of our humanness.

Following the theology of Karl Rahner we may accept the fact that demons are real. They are not, he tells us, hobgoblins, not abstract evil forces either. There is nothing abstract about them. They are, he writes, "Powers *of* the world (not independent of mankind) insofar as *this* world is a denial of God and a temptation to man" (emphasis his).

Every evil in the world, he says, is personally realized, or it is not evil. The personal demon is that which culpably closed one off from God in the usurpation of God's role.

They served their idols,
which became a snare for them.
They sacrificed their sons
and their daughters to demons (Ps 106:36-37).

We enter the desert to reflect, not to condemn. Condemnation accomplishes nothing. In the mirror of this desert of fear, we see our own rage reflected. We can pray "Father, forgive us, for we do not know what we are doing." But of course we know, we know very well. We may try, with Christ in the desert, to abandon ourselves to the care and mercy of the Father, knowing that Christ has robbed all oppressive Powers and Principalities of their effectiveness. The power that seems so real, of armies, tyrants, weapons and war, is only an arrogant sham. The only future that awaits us is God, and the reign of peace, justice and love. It is a future made possible by the fidelity of the little ones of the world.

The Desert of the Spirit

People not only long for national and international peace, they long for acceptance and a loving environment. They long for God. The best and worst of people long for God, irrespective of how untheologically they spell that longing. The hunger of the heart is just that: a hunger. It is not a hunger for something specific: a woman or a man, theology, a job. The unrelenting hunger is for All, for God. The worst desert is where that hunger is misunderstood or despised. To find oneself in a small country or city where the culture is dominated by a religion other than one's own is to find oneself in a desert. We have to admit humbly that religion has a tendency to dominate culture wherever it finds itself unchallenged. It lays a heavy hand on politics, education, lifestyle and recreation. Yet the Spirit of Jesus is amongst us as "one who serves," not dominates.

"Model" religious cities are corrupted by respectability. We are not allowed to be human, sinful and broken there. There are model Catholic, Mormon and Protestant cities. To be fully human is to be a forgiven sinner. Not to acknowledge human weakness, something model cities cannot endure, is a corruption of the spirit. It breeds hypocrisy. This pattern of corruption is evident wherever there are model cities. It matters not whether one is a Catholic in a Mormon city, a Mormon in a Catholic city, a Jew in Lebanon, a black in a Dutch Reformed suburb of Johannesburg, or an Anglican visiting the Vatican. Whether it be respectability, violence, apartheid or insularity, the result is the same: It is a testing of the spirit in one's personal desert. The intruder into such deserts receives that insolent stare which questions his or her salvation. We must be co-opted or driven out. At best we become lost people, patronized by cold tolerance. We confront the congealed indifference of finite understandings.

There is as much, perhaps vastly more, violence in the desert of religion as there is in the nuclear desert. It is more subtle because it is more spritual. It warps minds and hearts, setting people against their brothers and sisters, setting the individual against himself or herself.

When the longing for God and for religion as a visible and social expression of our relationship to God are confined to one narrow and fanatically defended aspect of truth, the longing turns on us and destroys us. Truth of its nature must be universal. What is known to be true and good in the religion of another must be revered and acceptable within one's own. Good works must be extended to all, irrespective of religious affiliation. Otherwise the heart is soiled since God is beyond all grasping. The demons which inhabit the desert of the spirit are vested interests, factions, prejudice, ignorance and misinformation. We do not have to pay homage to them. They can be overcome.

> *"You shall do homage to the Lord your God;*
> *him alone shall you adore"* (Mt 4:10).

What, in the place of citicism, do we have to offer one another? Only disinterested love and the willingness to be crucified. Should we experience misunderstanding, we have the power of Chirst to love that person, communist or capitalist, catholic, protestant, hispanic or anglo. There is only one mystery. It is the radical solitude from whence comes the Word of love through the genius of the Spirit. To find that solitude, ground of our being and desert of our purification, is our quest. There we find the Word whose joy is placed in us that our joy might be complete. There also we find our mission which is to establish the reign of justice, peace and love on the earth.

The scriptures tell us that it profits religious people nothing loving those who love them. The irreligious do as much. The think-alikes huddling together in endless self-affirmation are not worshipping God. Worship begins where our spirit is crucified by the love we have for others.

It is the irony of God, the only vengeance God knows, that we are saved by those we most depise. It is we who make them the *anawim,* the poor of God, the suffering servants. Our grudging tolerance and small acceptance open our hearts in spite of ourselves to the salvific pain we inflict on them. It is God's irony that saints are saved by sinners who humble them lest their accomplishments seduce their spirits. Yes, Christ alone saves us, but the instruments he uses are strange indeed. Those being saved need the thorn in the flesh. In the scandal of the divided churches, this is our only area of hope. We keep each other humble. Bigots refuse to accept obvious facts; pious fanatics swallow everything and think that they know everything; foolish people are obsessed by theologies they can neither accept nor reject. We are the perpetrators and victims of all of this. Who could possibly deliver us but Christ who loved the unlovable, forgave the unforgivable and continued to hope when everything was lost?

Rainer Maria Rilke wrote: "Everything terrible in us is, in its deepest being, something helpless asking for help." In the deserts of our troubled state, we choose to be like Christ, opting to be who and what we are, yet in a communion of love with all. A Celtic prayer puts it this way:

> *God, kindle in my heart within*
> *a flame of love to any neighbor,*
> *to my foe, to my friend, to my kindred all,*
> *to the brave, to the knave, to the thrall*
> *—O Son of the loveliest Mary—*
> *from the loftiest thing that lives*
> *to the Name that is highest of all.*

Now, we are ready for the mountain.

What To Do

Purpose: To expand consciousness and compassion.

Share: Physical deserts you have seen or visited.
The dry periods in your faith or prayerlife.
The demons of the desert: fears, obsessions, compulsions.

Music: Debussy, *La Mer Nocturnes,* Phillips 411 156-4.

Reflection: What did you learn from the dry spells?
Extend your compassion toward others.

End: Read aloud Hosea 2:16-35.

"The Old Man on the Mountain"

We still believe he's up there, the old man on the mountain, to be discovered on the high level of prayer in the exhilirating experience of some broad vision. And, in a sense, it's true.

> *Who can ascend the mountain of the LORD,*
> *or who may stand in his holy place* (Ps 24:3)?

In Hebrew parallelism mountain and holy place are one and the same.

> *You are enthroned in the holy place,*
> *O glory of Israel!* (Ps 22:4).

There are those who do not much like this vertical spirituality, feeling that it ignores the horizontal concern with others. They are complementary. The symbol of the mountain as the holy place is too ancient and universal to be false.

Every religion has its holy mountain. For the Jews there are Zion, Carmel and Sinai/Hored. For the people of the New Testament there are the Mount of Transfiguration, the mounts of Beatitudes, Calvary and Ascension. For the Japanese Mount Fugi is sacred; Kailas is sacred for the Nepalese. Greece has Olympus, Ireland has Croagh Patrick, Sri Lanka has Adam's Peak, the Plains Indians had the Black Hills and even so recent a religion as that of the Mormons has Hill Cumorah. This same phenomenon is discovered throughout South America and Africa. The mountain is the universal religious symbol. Irrespective of the religion to which we belong, we must climb the mountain of the Lord and stand in the holy place.

It is true that some primitive people seemed to worship the mountain itself as a god; merely to touch Kailas was to be forgiven, to encircle the mountain on pilgrimage was to be assured of salvation. The mountain, for the most part, was a symbol that revealed the power and presence of the mystery in people's lives.

The View

The first sight of the Tetons is an exhilirating and humbling experience. They are the kind of mountains that children draw: huge jagged peaks rising straight up from the valley floor. In Jackson Hole one can walk in close under their shadow. Here we find that perfect combination of natural phenomena which have moved religious consciousness since pre-history: desert, water, trees and mountain. Antelope inhabit the sagebrush desert. Conifers surround Jenny, Leigh and Jackson lakes. Out of the lakes rise the mountains. It is a place of great beauty, a place to bring one's troubles. The mountain meadows are covered with larkspur, lupines, blue harebells and mountain bluebells. Mule deer and moose may be seen in early spring and on the lakes there are trumpeter swans. Wild raspberries and thimbleberries grow along the mountain paths and are delicious to eat. And when we are thirsty it is safe to drink from Cascade Creek.

On my first visit to the Tetons I was accompanied by a friend, Michael. He was a troubled person, obsessed by scruples that had developed from a rigid moralistic upbringing. He opened my eyes to the mountains and cleansed my consciousness in their regard. He had been living on the edge of another desert, within sight of other mountains. He was somewhat unkempt, not by design but by the fact that being kempt (combed) was not a value that occured to him. Desert dust lay embedded in the lines of his hollow cheeks, but he was a God-seeker.

I had thought that by taking him out and showing him a little of civilization for a couple of weeks I might rescue him from the squalor of his surroundings. I had much to learn. As he saw it, the troubles of life, such as eeking out a meager living in harsh surroundings, are the measure of a person. They push one to the limits of human endurance revealing what is possible and what is impossible. They keep one honest.

There was nothing soft or self-indulgent about Michael; he had no room for illusions. Very quietly he pointed out to me that my concept of civilization was built on illusions: illusions of what makes one happy, illusions of power and wealth and control, of fear of enemies, of ambition and moralistic humbug. His own mountain had lifted his eyes from the dirt, but this trip held the danger of making him less of a person.

"So this is civilization," he said, his eyes on the garish billboards and the unaccustomed traffic. "People huddled together in cities because they fear death."

"People huddle together for security, and because they have a desperate need to be loved," I replied. "And cities have a good many things going for them—the fruits of the human spirit—symphony concerts, ballet, museums, art galleries, lots of things."

"Those are merely cultural things," he said quietly, "and for the few. The poor cannot afford them. There is nothing civilized about cities."

When we arrived at the mountains he sat on his heels staring at the pebbles in the clear water of Jenny Lake. It was October and we had the place to ourselves. All the hurried tourists had packed up and returned to the cities. He lifted up his eyes to the mountains: "Now, this is civil," he said.

When we stand at the lake's edge and listen to the low rumble of the falls on the mountains' face, or watch the water lapping at our feet, we know "whence help comes to us" (Ps 121). It isn't a matter of searching for the mystery hidden behind the appearances, but of seeing the mystery revealed in the appearances. The world becomes transparent. We sense the oneness of all things. The sights, the sounds, the essences of things, the mountains and ourselves are wrapped in the oneness of the God of peace and love. At just such a moment we come to know the Source of our longing. Longing at its deepest level is always for God, and our troubles lead us there.

Our hunger has to do with infinity. "We are made for you," wrote Augustine, "and our hearts are restless until they rest in you." The human heart will never be satisfied with what is merely finite. Not that it cannot be distracted, but that it cannot be fulfilled. The finite mind has finite understanding and fears the challenge to that understanding lest it lose it. This is why we cling so desperately to the finite. We see it in angry people, in military solutions to social problems, in religious fanatics. But in a moment of wonder before the beauty of the mountains we know that an intuitive mind is open to infinite understandings.

The mountains awaken us to the solitude within, the hushed spaces of the spirit where ordinary people live with the mystery of life. This solitude of each person is the sanctuary of our dignity. It is here that we make the unending journey toward our roots in the mystery of God. We are challenged by the danger and risk of having anything at all to do with mystery. We fear the darkness of pure faith and trust that is required of us. Our inner solitude is as vast as the outer reach of space. We confront both. With our unique self, culture and religion we dwell where both solitudes meet. In faith and trust, we leave behind us our history, security, self and culture when we plan to climb the mountain of the Lord.

We confront the outer spaces, the heavens proclaiming the glory of God, and wonder what we might be that God should be mindful of us. We also confront our inner space, the depths of our rootedness in God. Confronting both opens our heart to the infinite. We come to know that we are always greater than anything we can know about ourselves. The mountain vastness opens us to this intuition, and the wisdom of the heart grows. We do not want anything from the mountain or from God. We want to be still and see that God is God. We do not want the mountain or God to be anything they are not.

As we walk slowly along the lake's edge, our eyes soak up the beauty of pebbles polished by ancient glaciers, old gnarled tree roots and worn granite boulders. We pick up a piece of driftwood and will bring it home, but it will be out of place there and lose its meaning. There are buttercups, scarlet paintbrush, yellow senecio and patches of cinquefoil. We search and gaze, not wanting to miss anything, and our spirits are filled with joy.

The mountains belong to those who love them. There are many viewpoints. There is one view for those who live on the flatlands, whose mentality is formed by flatland living. The world of the flatlanders is merely a home with a view. Without reflection, their view of the mountains is indulgent. For those who enter the mountain solitudes there is an altogether other view, one of fear and joy, of mystery and awe. For them, as Isaiah would have it, "the mountains dance."

There is fear; in the mountain solitude we confront our troubles. We begin to ask the hard questions. There are few, if any, answers to the things which bother us. Were there answers, the vast spaces would cease to be a solitude. There would be no more mystery, no fulfillment of human longing, no way out. It is in the longing, not in the answers, that we find growth. What a good question does is open us up to infinity, wash our eyes that we might gaze on mystery. But all answers are finite. They are cheap possessions. The greatest accomplishment is to realize that the Mystery of Being, the Sourceless Source, can never be grasped and hoarded as if it were a possession or an answer. It is out of all possessions and finite answers that God is calling us through our troubles to experience a total self-transcendence. The fulfillment of our longing will be realized, not when our troubles cease but when we surrender in trust to the Mystery at the source of our life.

When we surrender the depths of our hearts to the mountain solitude, we find ourselves at the center of the mystery. We come to the disturbing insight that mystery is the essential reality of existence and of our being. It is not anything which can be measured, assessed, accounted for or controlled. We ask questions because the mystery permeates every moment of our history, and we long for some form of clarification. Dogmatic statements have their place, but they are finite measurements. Few people realize that such measurements are only symbols which invite us further into the mystery. They stop short at appearances. The mountain prompts the kind of questions which goad us toward infinity: Where did it all begin? Where shall it end? What meaning does my life have? What must I do with my life? Why am I troubled?

These questions, and more, humble the spirit and cleanse our minds for the moment of intuition. Insight is hard to come by on the flatland where our minds are filled with the problems of everyday living. In the mountains, the intuition is more than a solution to our problems, it is a creative and growth-filled moment of union with the problems of everyday living. In the mountains, the intuition is more than a solution to our problems, it is a creative and growth-filled moment of union with mystery. God is present and life has meaning despite the troubles.

Holy mountains are the revelatory place of the divine because they have something of the mystery and stability of God. They bear up unmoved under the seasons. They are trustworthy. Even when neglected, they remain there awaiting our return. They are silent with the silence of wisdom, unyielding in power, uncompromising in truth. They dwarf not only our bodies, but our spirits too; they make us humble. Compared to them, our life is as the life of a gnat. They are full of life and nurture life. Should a nuclear holocaust destroy the world, the mountains will remain, silent and asleep in winter's snows, shedding cascades of tears in spring, laughing in their rockfalls in summer. The mountains will survive and bring back life again from their tears and fire. From the mountains have always come the covenants of peace.

The Ascent

The water is calm on Jenny Lake today. It reflects the mountain just as a calm mind reflects God. But if the mind is disturbed, God disappears and we must build bridges of compassion to reach out again.

We cross the bridge which spans the overflow at the south end of the lake. We are aware of many things: the smell of stone under the hot sun, the wisps of fog at the higher elevations, the murmur of water, a distant eagle's flight. They are all words within the Word of God. They are not some reality or activity in the world, but the activity of the world as the world lives out the life of the Word. They are theophanies demanding a response: that we be the little ones learning the reality of the sacred, learning to be gentle. To be sacred is to be set apart form all forms of greed. The mountain calls us to rid ourselves of all obsessions, addictions and phobias, of all narrowness and pettiness. They call us to worship:

> *Great is the lord and wholly to be praised*
> *in the city of our God.*
> *His holy mountain, fairest of heights,*
> *is the joy of all the earth* (Ps 48:1).

The joy arising from the sight of the mountains, and the excitement, must never be separated from reverence for the mountain itself, from what it is and what it can do. The amateur climber—the novice in the ways of the spirit—has oftentimes a sense of enthusiasm combined with a lack of reverence. It all seems so simple. Without thought of hazards the novice may get killed. Hardly a year passes that one or a few are not killed on the Tetons. Lacking food or adequate clothing, some have been caught in sudden snowstorms and have perished. Last year a climber slipped on the Teton glacier and was stabbed to death by his own ice axe. Rockfalls have claimed others. But the seasoned climbers frighten all of us by their commitment and the intensity of their self-transcendence. They ascend by routes for which we have no courage. In some strange manner they experience themselves being taken up as the mountain falls away beneath them.

The climb is a metaphor of our ascent toward God; the mountain is a symbol of God. For the time being it is not reaching the summit that matters. Gregory of Nyssa wrote: "He who climbs must climb forever." What matters is the decision to walk in the way. The spirituality of our ascent begins with a decision, not with the first step. The decision to make the ascent, to climb out of our troubles, accepts the possibility of failing. But it includes a protest against the many selfish neuroses of flatland living. If we must be put to the test, it should be in the hazards of self-transcendence rather than in the hazards of self-indulgence.

The ascent to God should never be seen as a burden placed upon us. If we see it as such, it will inevitably lead to boredom and despair. Not that the climb is without troubles, but that its meaning is found in hope. Where the flatlander sees only burdens and obstacles, the people of decision see the route. By their decision they cut themselves off from all retreat. We may run into something beyond our capacity on the ascent. The sense of being trapped in the wall may flow over us: We cannot ascend, we cannot return. Exhaustion or the temperature may overwhelm us. In the end we come to know that we live by hope, not by accomplishments. Hope springs alive in our spirit; something small but delightful will happen. It might be a marmot scurrying for cover, the sight or squeak of the pikas, an unexpected view of Cirque Lake or Lake Solitude. Something will trigger the moment of amazement. This mountain is the way and the ultimate hazard. It reaches from earth to heaven. It is the symbol of our way out from imprisonment in the finite. Without it, the world is without hope.

The mountain gives itself to us. Neither mountain nor God are there to be conquered. We do not compete with God so as to conquer divinity. We do not compete with the mountain. To do so would be a fool's game. On the climb we compete with ourselves so as to maintain an inner calm and rid ourselves of tension. Our minds and muscles remain relaxed so as to be free and unhurried. On the mountain of God, we never push ourselves or make our pulse beat. Just as everything is fast on the flatland, everything is slow on the mountain: the hand grasping the granite, the lifeline which is reached out to others, the search for toeholds. The movements of the ascent is stillness, not sudden lunges. The mountain will kill those who ignore the dangers. It is a harmony of inner and outer strengths and energies. This is the manner of the spiritual journey of ordinary people.

Our bodies must not fight the mountain, nor must our spirits. Fanatics make poor mountain climbers. Body and spirit reverence the mystery and interplay with it. We never forget that it is the mountain itself which called us and allows us to climb by providing toeholds for the ascent. The call to climb, our response, the route and our patient ascent in the route are all the work of the one mystery which is "the Way, and the Truth and the Life."

The call ordinary people have received is to create their own essential being. The ascent is the work of that creation. But we must not ascend for self-serving purposes. An ascent which ignores others on the mountain is selfish. Our experience of trouble and our transcendence of it is an admonishment to be aware of others and to reach out to them. The climb is not an end in itself, though there are those who see it that way. Climbers should not be full of self-congratulation at their technique and achievement. The mountain is not an excuse for triumphalism in religion. The humble climber will show others the way, and having reached the summit will return, not to boast, but to show that he or she has become a changed person. This is the creation of one's essential being. We freely admit our fears, needs and failures. We also celebrate the glory of it all, and convey this to others lest they falter on the way.

No one will belittle us if we lose courage and ask for help. All know that it would be a mistake to dramatize the ascent: the fears, the exhaustion and the pain of people climbing out of the dark valley are all too real. We are in the presence of death and hardly know if we shall ever descend again. We feel, humbly enough, that we are fortunate to be alive, to have come as far as we have come, pushing one foot before the other.

We seek God in this metaphorical ascent, the fulfillment of our infinite longing. We also seek ourselves within the being of God. But there are barriers: crevasses, outcrops, slippery glaciers, and worry, anxiety, uncertainty and pressure from friends who say that we cannot or should not do it. We must ascend past these barriers, no matter how helpless we feel. Only then shall we experience ourselves as called. The very thought of difficulties is itself a barrier which restricts our freedom. These barriers must be torn down by our willingness to sacrifice ourselves. There is no other way. It is this willingness which sets us free. The inner solitude of our spirit combined with this outer wilderness enables us to arrive at this self-offering. Tourists who want thrills on the mountain do not belong there. There was one such among the Lord's disciples and the scandal of Calvary killed him. Self-offering was too great a barrier.

There are times when we wonder if it makes any sense. The wind blows, cutting our faces. Our fingers are numb. The clouds do not stand still in awe of our sacrifice. The wildlife scatter in fear of our presence. Nerves are frayed. Yet the climb remains symbolic of our lifelong search for a spiritual meaning to our existence. The climb is inevitable, or life will be devoid of purpose. We do what we came into the world to do: climb toward a summit which has neither profit nor power for a flat-lander. We have our secret wisdom, that a thousand miles of flatland has not as much interest for the human spirit as does one small hill rising above it. We must climb. The soles of our shoes may be thin, dancing on the mountain, but our decision is firm and our hope intact. We climb upright, face to face with the mountain, voice to voice with the music of the universe.

The Summit

There is no "Old Man" on the summit. There is the relaxation of sitting in our perspiration and enjoying the view and the cool breeze. This in itself is rest for the spirit, being still and contemplative. There is however an insight: The Old Man is in the face of the rock. God is in the hazards of the way, the way being vastly superior to the attainment of the summit. Troubled people realize that they have accomplished what they set out to do. They discover that the Mystery was with them all along. They look back on their lives and know that God was there in tears and joy, in frustration and frayed nerves, in celebrations and failure, in unexpected delights, in barriers and the transcendence of barriers. To finally come to live this union is the purpose of life and of life's journey.

Our protests and troubles finally cease. The barriers come down. There is nothing now between us and the vast expanse of heaven.

> *Shatter now this beggar's bowl;*
> *put out the lamp of this persistent seeker.*
> *Hold my hands, raise me from*
> *this still-gathering heap of your gifts*
> *into the open spaces*
> *of your uncrowded presence* (A Prayer from India).

What To Do

Purpose:　　To reflect on our journey toward God.

Discuss:　　Why it is that people love the ocean, mountains, lakes—making them symbols of God.
Why "the view from the top" is special.
Places you have been that brought you close to God.

Music:　　Mozart, Symphony 41 *"Jupiter."*

Quiet Time:　Center within.
You do not compete with God, or God with you!
Surrender to the Mystery.
Allow yourself to be taken up.
God has always been with you,
even in the worst of times.

End:　　Read aloud the account of the Transfiguration, Luke 9:28-36.